New Edition

PRE-INTERMEDIATE

Language in use

Self-Study Workbook
with answer key

ADRIAN DOFF & CHRISTOPHER JONES

CAMBRIDGE
UNIVERSITY PRESS

PUBLISHED BY THE PRESS SYNDICATE OF THE UNIVERSITY OF CAMBRIDGE
The Pitt Building, Trumpington Street, Cambridge, United Kingdom

CAMBRIDGE UNIVERSITY PRESS
The Edinburgh Building, Cambridge CB2 2RU, UK
40 West 20th Street, New York, NY 10011–4211, USA
10 Stamford Road, Oakleigh, VIC 3166, Australia
Ruiz de Alarcón 13, 28014 Madrid, Spain
Dock House, The Waterfront, Cape Town 8001, South Africa

http://www.cambridge.org

First published 1991
New edition 2000
Fifth printing 2001

Printed in the United Kingdom at the University Press, Cambridge

ISBN 0 521 77405 5 Self-study Workbook with Answer Key
ISBN 0 521 77406 3 Self-study Workbook
ISBN 0 521 77407 1 Classroom Book
ISBN 0 521 77404 7 Teacher's Book
ISBN 0 521 77403 9 Class Cassette Set
ISBN 0 521 77402 0 Self-study Cassette
ISBN 0 521 65461 0 Video (PAL)
ISBN 0 521 65460 2 Video (NTSC)

Contents

To the student

This Workbook contains exercises for you to do on your own.

Like the Classroom Book, it has units and Study Pages.

The units contain:
- homework exercises
- a listening activity
- a list of new words.

The Study Pages contain:
- a progress test
- a phrasebook exercise
- a writing activity.

At the end of the book, there is a Final Review test.

The Workbook has a Self-study Cassette. You will need this for the Listening exercises in each unit. The tapescripts are at the back of the book.

The Workbook pages look like this:

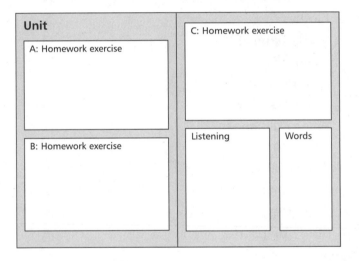

Homework exercises
These give extra practice in the main grammar or vocabulary of the unit. There are usually three homework exercises.

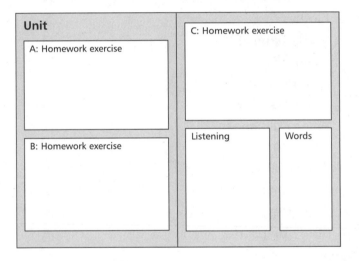 **Listening**
Each unit has a short listening activity.

Words
Some useful vocabulary from the unit. You write the words in your own language. You can also add your own words.

Study pages	
Check your progress	Phrase-book
page 1	

Writing

page 2

Check your progress
A progress test on the last two units and Study Pages in the Classroom Book.

Phrasebook
This has phrases from the Classroom Book exercise. You write the phrases in your own language.

Writing
Write paragraphs using language from earlier units.

Guide to units

	Self-study Workbook	Classroom Book
1 **Things people do**	Grammar exercises Listening: *The best time of the day*	Saying what people do; saying how often you do things; talking about facts **Grammar:** Present simple tense; frequency expressions
2 **Family and friends**	Vocabulary exercises Listening: *Relatives*	Talking about family and other relationships **Vocabulary:** Family and friends; love and marriage
Study pages A	Check your progress Phrasebook Writing: *Joining sentences*	**Focus on ...** Personal data **Pronunciation:** Unusual words (1) **Phrasebook:** Introductions **Consolidation:** Possessives: *'s* and *s'*; *awake* and *wake up* **Review**
3 **Talking about places**	Grammar exercises Listening: *Rooms and flats*	Describing places; saying what there is; asking about facilities **Grammar:** *There is/are*; *have/has got*
4 **On the move**	Vocabulary exercises Listening: *Trip to Stonehenge*	Describing regular journeys; talking about public transport; asking for travel information **Vocabulary:** Arriving and leaving; ways of travelling; adjectives; times and costs
Study pages B	Check your progress Phrasebook Writing: *Punctuation*	**Focus on ...** Where things are **Pronunciation:** Small words (1) **Phrasebook:** Buying a ticket **Consolidation:** *early*, *in/on time*, *late*; the time of day **Review**
5 **Talking about now**	Grammar exercises Listening: *We're busy*	Talking about things happening 'now' and 'around now'; describing scenes **Grammar:** Present continuous tense; *There is/are* + *-ing*
6 **Food and drink**	Vocabulary exercises Listening: *Polish dishes*	Describing dishes and ingredients; saying what you eat; buying food **Vocabulary:** Food and drink; containers
Study pages C	Check your progress Phrasebook Writing: *Reference*	**Focus on ...** Likes and dislikes **Pronunciation:** Clusters (1) **Phrasebook:** In a café **Consolidation:** Simple and continuous; *get* **Review**

	Self-study Workbook	Classroom Book
7 The past	Grammar exercises Listening: *A man and a penguin*	Talking about past events; saying when things happened **Grammar:** Past simple tense; time expressions
8 A place to live	Vocabulary exercises Listening: *Favourite rooms*	Talking about houses **Vocabulary:** Houses and flats; locations; rooms and furniture; adjectives
Study pages D	Check your progress Phrasebook Writing: *Joining ideas*	Focus on ... *Both* and *neither* Pronunciation: Small words (2) Phrasebook: Finding a room Consolidation: Past time expressions; *very, quite ...* Review
9 I've done it!	Grammar exercises Listening: *What has happened?*	Talking about things that have just happened; asking about preparations **Grammar:** Present perfect tense; past participles
10 Clothes	Vocabulary exercises Listening: *Working clothes*	Talking about clothes; buying clothes; saying when you wear things **Vocabulary:** Clothes; colours, sizes and prices
Study pages E	Check your progress Phrasebook Writing: *Sequence (1)*	Focus on ... *Mine, yours ...* Pronunciation : Unusual words (2) Phrasebook: Paying for things Consolidation: Present perfect and Past simple; *'s* Review
11 Quantity	Grammar exercises Listening: *A healthy diet*	Talking about quantity; saying there is too much and not enough **Grammar:** *a/some/any*; quantity expressions; *How much/many ...?*; *too much/many* and *not enough*
12 How do you feel?	Vocabulary exercises Listening: *Ouch!*	Talking about aches and pains; saying what you do when you're ill; going to the doctor **Vocabulary:** aches and pains; parts of the body; remedies; doctors and medicine
Study pages F	Check your progress Phrasebook Writing: *Lists*	Focus on ... *For* and *since* Pronunciation: Small words (3) Phrasebook: Making an appointment Consolidation: *a little, a few, very little, very few*; *well* Review

	Self-study Workbook	Classroom Book
13 **What will happen?**	Grammar exercises Listening: *Giving blood*	Making predictions; giving advice **Grammar:** *will*, *won't* and *might*; *will probably* and *probably won't*
14 **About town**	Vocabulary exercises Listening: *Living in London*	Where to go in towns; describing shops and restaurants; giving directions **Vocabulary:** Places to go in towns; shopping; direction prepositions
Study pages G	Check your progress Phrasebook Writing: *Reason and contrast*	**Focus on …** *When* and *if* **Pronunciation:** Unusual words (3) **Phrasebook:** Buying a ticket (2) **Consolidation:** Short answers; two-word verbs Review
15 **Comparing things**	Grammar exercises Listening: *The most and the fewest*	Making comparisons; expressing preferences; describing outstanding features **Grammar:** Comparative adjectives; *than*; superlative adjectives
16 **Free time**	Vocabulary exercises Listening: *Rock climbing*	Talking about leisure activities; explaining how sports are played **Vocabulary:** Leisure activities; enjoyment and ability; sports
Study pages H	Check your progress Phrasebook Writing: *Sequence (2)*	**Focus on …** Ability **Pronunciation:** Clusters (2) **Phrasebook:** Asking where **Consolidation:** *more*, *less* and *fewer*; *go* and *play* Review
17 **Rules and advice**	Grammar exercises Listening: *Radio phone-in*	Giving rules; talking about obligation; giving advice **Grammar:** *have to* and *don't have to*; *can* and *can't*; *must* and *mustn't*; *should* and *shouldn't*
18 **A day's work**	Vocabulary exercises Listening: *A security guard*	Talking about jobs; saying why you would(n't) enjoy different jobs; describing a career **Vocabulary:** Names of jobs; features of jobs; stages of a career
Study pages I	Check your progress Phrasebook Writing: *Letter writing*	**Focus on …** *Someone*, *anyone* **Pronunciation:** Words with *-ion* **Phrasebook:** Renting things **Consolidation:** Verbs with prepositions; *do* Review

	Self-study Workbook	Classroom Book
19 **Telling stories**	Grammar exercises Listening: *The wedding video*	Talking about past events and their circumstances; telling stories; describing a scene in the past **Grammar:** Past continuous tense; Past simple tense; *when* and *while*
20 **People**	Vocabulary exercises Listening: *Family picture*	Describing people's physical appearance; saying roughly how old people are; describing people's characters **Vocabulary:** Physical characteristics; age; character adjectives
Study pages J	Check your progress Phrasebook Writing: *Relative clauses (1)*	**Focus on ...** Nationalities **Pronunciation:** Unusual words (4) **Phrasebook:** Personal questions **Consolidation:** *while* and *during*; *with* Review
21 **Future plans**	Grammar exercises Listening: *Plans for the evening*	Talking about intentions and plans; talking about future arrangements **Grammar:** *going to*; *will*; Present continuous tense; future time expressions
22 **Around the world**	Vocabulary exercises Listening: *Living in a hot climate*	Saying where things are in the world; saying what places are like; asking about tourist destinations **Vocabulary:** Countries and continents; geographical features and location; climate
Study pages K	Check your progress Phrasebook Writing: *Relative clauses (2)*	**Focus on ...** *Nothing, no one, nowhere* **Pronunciation:** Consonant links **Phrasebook:** Arranging to meet **Consolidation:** Using the Present continuous; *It's ...* Review
23 **Past and present**	Grammar exercises Listening: *Have you ever ...?*	Talking about changes; talking about experiences **Grammar:** Present perfect tense; *still* and *yet*; *ever* and *never*
24 **Arts and entertainment**	Vocabulary exercises Listening: *TV survey*	Talking about cultural events; talking about TV programmes **Vocabulary:** Art and culture; writers, artists and performers; television programmes

Final review

1 Things people do

A Positive and negative

Jane is completely different from her parents. For example:

She reads magazines, but she doesn't read newspapers.
They read newspapers, but they don't read magazines.

I	smoke.
We	
They	don't smoke.

He	smokes.
She	doesn't smoke.

Complete these sentences about Jane and her parents.

1 She watches news programmes, but she doesn't watch old films.
   They ....

2 They go to the theatre, but they don't go to parties.
   She ....

3 She uses a computer, but she doesn't use a typewriter.
   ....

4 They smoke, but they don't drink wine.
   ....

5 She plays basketball, but she doesn't play chess.
   ....

6 They like cats, but they don't like dogs.
   ....

B On Saturdays

What do you do on Saturdays? Do you

– visit friends?   – go shopping?   – cook a meal?
– work?   – play football? – go to bed late?

Write about yourself, using frequency expressions from the table. Examples:

I often visit friends.   *I don't usually cook a meal.*

1 ....

2 ....

3 ....

4 ....

5 ....

6 ....

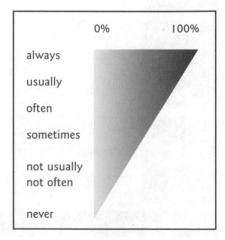

	0%	100%
always		
usually		
often		
sometimes		
not usually not often		
never		

Now write about two other things that you do (or don't do) on Saturdays.

7 ....

8 ....

C Asking Wh- questions

Write questions using question words from the box.

How much	What	What time
When	Where	Why

1 Does it cost £5? £8? £15?

   How much does it cost?

2 Do they live in Rome? Paris? Tokyo?

   Where

3 Do crocodiles eat fish? plants? people?

   ....

4 Does she park her car in a garage? in the street? in a car park?

   ....

5 Do you have lunch at 1 o'clock? 1.30? 2 o'clock?

   ....

6 Do you want £10? £100? £1,000?

   ....

7 Does he walk to work because he enjoys it? because he hasn't got a car? for the exercise?

   ....

8 Do you use English at work? at home? on holiday?

   ....

Listening: *The best time of the day*

🔲 Three people talk about the time of day they like best. Listen and complete the table. Write two things each speaker does.

Speaker 1

Best time: ....

Things she does: ....

....

Speaker 2

Best time: ....

Things he does: ....

....

Speaker 3

Best time: ....

Things she does: ....

....

Which speaker

– is a student? ....   – works in an office? ....

– is married? ....

Words

Write these words in your language.

classical music ....

jazz ....

concert ....

go out ....

come round (to my flat) ....

make a bed ....

send (a card) ....

Other words

....

....

....

....

A Family tree

Complete this family tree with words from the box.
One of the words isn't used. Which one?

☑ mother   ☐ son
☐ father   ☐ daughter
☐ grandmother   ☐ uncle
☑ grandfather   ☐ aunt
☑ granddaughter   ☑ father-in-law
☐ grandson   ☐ mother-in-law
☑ brother   ☐ brother-in-law
☐ sister   ☐ sister-in-law
☐ cousin   ☐ son-in-law
☐ niece   ☐ daughter-in-law
☐ nephew

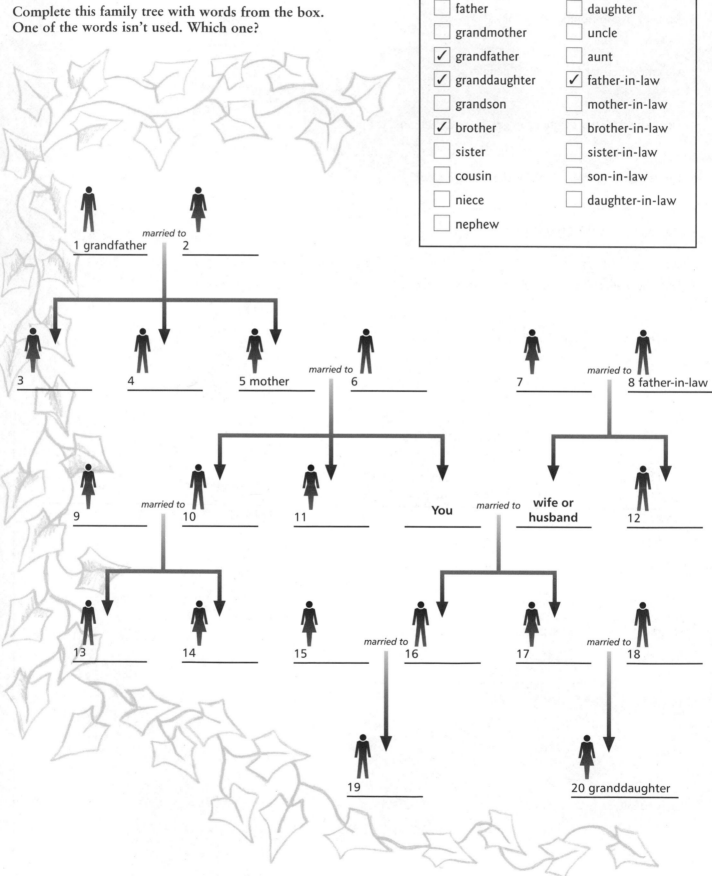

1 grandfather · *married to* · 2 _____

3 _____ · 4 _____ · 5 mother · *married to* · 6 _____ · 7 _____ · *married to* · 8 father-in-law

9 _____ · *married to* · 10 _____ · 11 _____ · **You** · *married to* · **wife or husband** · 12 _____

13 _____ · 14 _____ · 15 _____ · 16 _____ · *married to* · 17 _____ · 18 _____ · *married to*

19 _____

20 granddaughter

B Relatives, friends and neighbours

Write about two of these people.

1 a relative
2 a friend (maybe a flat-mate or room-mate)
3 a neighbour

Include answers to these questions,
and add any other information you like.

> My room-mate Leo is 20. We share a room at
> the university. He studies chemistry, and he also
> works in a restaurant at weekends. He's got a
> girlfriend called Claire. I think they're engaged.

How old
is he/she?

Is he/she single?
engaged? married?
divorced?

Where does
he/she live?

Where does
he/she work or study?

1 ....

....

....

2 ....

....

....

Listening: *Relatives*

Three people talk about their relatives. For each relative,
find three differences from the sentences below.

1 My grandmother is 95. She lives with us in London. She can't walk
  but she still reads a lot.

  a ....

  b ....

  c ....

2 My brother is a lorry driver. He travels all over Europe. He always
  brings back presents from the countries he visits. I think he has
  a boring job.

  a ....

  b ....

  c ....

3 My uncle sells computers and he's very rich. He has two houses
  with swimming pools, and he goes on expensive holidays. I don't
  like him because he's mean.

  a ....

  b ....

  c ....

Words

Write these words in your language.

nice   ....

interesting   ....

travel   ....

receive   ....

get engaged   ....

get married   ....

meet   ....

die   ....

alone   ....

Other words

....

....

....

....

....

Check your progress

1 Here's a number, a date and a time. Write them in words.

365 ....

15 Jan 1999 ....

11.45 ....

2 Whose bedrooms? Fill the gaps with possessive forms.

> My parents sleep in the green room, and my sister sleeps in the yellow room. Harry sleeps in the blue room, and the children sleep in the red room.

a The green room is .... bedroom.

b The yellow room is .... bedroom.

c The blue room is .... bedroom.

d The red room is .... bedroom.

3 Fill the gaps with the opposites of the words in *italics*.

a I'm not .... I'm *awake*!

b I *go to sleep* at 11.00 and I .... at 7.00.

c They *go to bed* late, but they .... late too.

d OK. .... and have a quick shower, and then you can *get dressed* again.

4 Complete the conversation. Use the Present simple.

A *Do you* .... (you/work/Cambridge?)

B Yes. .... (work/bookshop)

A And your wife? .... (where/work?)

B She .... (work/university)

A Really? .... (what/teach?)

B She .... (not teach)

She .... (work/library)

5 Complete the table.

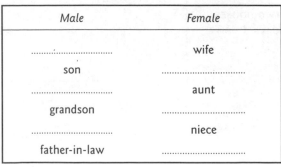

Male	Female
....	wife
son	....
....	aunt
grandson	....
....	niece
father-in-law	....

Phrasebook

Write these conversations in your language.

....

....

....

....

....

....

....

....

Writing *Joining sentences*

1 Look at these examples.

I don't have a brother. I have two sisters.
I don't have a brother *but* I have two sisters.

One sister is older than me. The other one is younger.
One sister is older than me *and* the other one is younger.

My older sister is married. She lives in London.
My older sister is married *and* lives in London.

2 These paragraphs have too many sentences. Join some of them together, so that each paragraph has *four* sentences.

I have no brothers or sisters. I have two cousins. One of them is younger than me. The other one is older. The younger one is 19. He has just started university. The older one is married. She lives with her family in Australia.

I have

I have two uncles. One is retired. He lives in Scotland. The other lives in London. He has two children. One is eight. The other is ten.

I have

3 Now write a short paragraph about people in your family.

3 | Talking about places

A Two descriptions

Here are pictures of a hotel bedroom and reception area. Write about them using *has got* and *there is/are*.

The bedroom
....
....
....
....
....
....

In the reception area
....
....
....
....
....
....

Has got	There is/are
The room has got a table.	There's a table in the room.
It's got four chairs.	There are four chairs.

B Not a good place for a holiday

These hotel guests aren't happy. Fill the gaps with *hasn't got*, *haven't got*, *there isn't* and *there aren't*.

The room hasn't got a window.
The rooms haven't got balconies.

There isn't a table.
There aren't any chairs.

The rooms **haven't got** phones.

.... a TV in my room.

.... a bar.

.... any chairs on the balconies.

The bathrooms .... windows.

.... any newspapers or magazines.

The swimming pool .... any water in it!

My room .... a toilet.

C Asking questions

Rewrite these questions using *Have/Has ... got ...?*

1 Is there a phone in your office?

....

2 Are there carpets in the classrooms?

....

3 Are there any trees in Antarctica?

....

Now rewrite these questions using *Is/Are there ...?*

4 Has this town got a university?

....

5 Has France got any mountains?

....

6 Has the village got any shops?

....

<table>
<tr><td>Has France got any mountains?</td></tr>
<tr><td>Have the rooms got balconies?</td></tr>
<tr><td>Is there a hotel in this town?</td></tr>
<tr><td>Are there any lakes in Egypt?</td></tr>
</table>

Listening: *Rooms and flats*

Here are some advertisements in the paper for rooms and flats.
(*Furnished* = it has furniture.)

A **ROOM** near city centre. Furnished.

B **ROOM to rent**. Ground floor.

C **FURNISHED FLAT**. One room, bathroom, kitchen.

D **LARGE FLAT**. 3rd floor. Near city centre.

E **FURNISHED FLAT**. 3 rooms, large balconies.

1 ▭ Listen to the two conversations. Which rooms or flats are they talking about?

   1 ....   2 ....

2 Listen again and complete the sentences.

   1 This is a small .... on the .... floor.

   It's got ....

   ....

   The bathroom is ....

   2 This is a large .... on the .... floor.

   It's got ....

   ....

   There isn't a ....

   It's by ....

Words

Write these words in your language.

fax machine ....

reception desk ....

blackboard ....

ashtray ....

thick ....

carpet ....

unfortunately ....

share (v.) ....

unusual ....

business trip ....

Other words

....

....

....

....

....

4 On the move

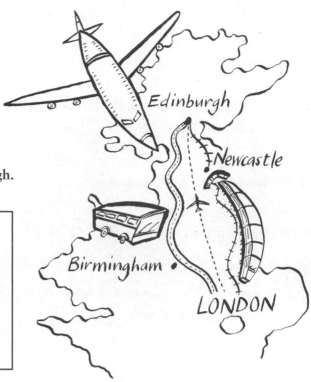

A Train, bus and plane

Someone describes the train journey from London to Edinburgh.
Can you match the first and second halves of the sentences?

~~I always go~~	the early morning train.
It costs	at about half past ten.
I usually catch	about four hours.
It leaves Kings Cross Station	~~by train~~.
It arrives at Edinburgh	at 6.25.
The whole journey takes	£65 return.

I always go by train. It costs
....

....

....

Now write about *either* the bus journey *or* the plane journey from
London to Edinburgh. Use the notes in the boxes.

....

....

....

....

PLANE
From Heathrow. £80 return. Morning. Leaves 7.40. Arrives 8.45.

BUS
From Victoria Bus Station. £45 return. Morning. Leaves 6.00. Arrives 3.00.

B Adjectives

Five people talk about public transport. Which *two* adjectives go best with each remark?

1 They always come on time, but the seats are very hard, especially on a long journey.

2 I can never find a seat, especially in the mornings, and they stop at every little station on the way.

3 They don't cost very much, but people say they have a lot of accidents.

4 The tickets cost a lot, but they have lovely big, soft seats.

5 Sometimes they come and sometimes they don't, so very few people use them.

comfortable
uncomfortable
cheap
expensive
fast
slow
safe
dangerous
empty
crowded
reliable
unreliable

1 ....

2 ....

3 ....

4 ....

5 ....

C Questions

Sally wants to visit her friend, who lives in Grandville. She phones and asks how to get there. Read the text, then look at the friend's answers. What are Sally's questions?

1 Q *How can I get to Grandville?*

A By bus, train or car.

2 Q *What*

A By train.

3 Q ....

A About £35.

4 Q ....

A About four hours.

5 Q ....

A At 8.05 in the morning.

6 Q ....

A At about 12.00.

7 Q ....

A By taxi.

You can get to Grandville by bus, train or car, but the best way to get there is by train. It costs about £35, and it takes about four hours. The train leaves at 8.05 in the morning, and arrives at about 12.00. You can get to my house from the station by taxi.

Listening: *Trip to Stonehenge*

A tourist in London wants to know how to get to Stonehenge.

▢ **Listen and fill the gaps.**

Stonehenge is .... from London.

The best way to go there is ....

It takes .... to get there, and

costs ....

You can't get there by train because ....

....

You can also .... That costs

about ....

Words

Write these words in your language.

fly (v.) ....

flight ....

bus terminal ....

convenient ....

weekdays ....

journey ....

pleasant ....

underground ....

not far ....

ferry boat ....

Other words

....

....

....

B Study pages

Check your progress

1 Where are they?

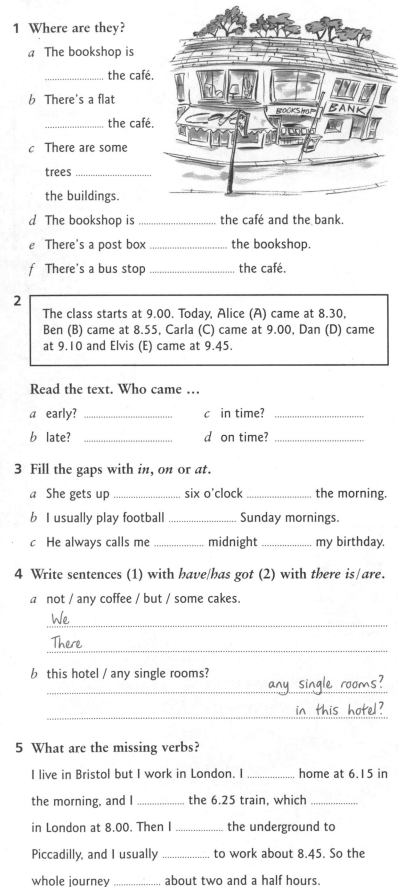

a The bookshop is

.... the café.

b There's a flat

.... the café.

c There are some

trees ....

the buildings.

d The bookshop is .... the café and the bank.

e There's a post box .... the bookshop.

f There's a bus stop .... the café.

2

> The class starts at 9.00. Today, Alice (A) came at 8.30, Ben (B) came at 8.55, Carla (C) came at 9.00, Dan (D) came at 9.10 and Elvis (E) came at 9.45.

Read the text. Who came ...

a early? .... *c* in time? ....

b late? .... *d* on time? ....

3 Fill the gaps with *in*, *on* or *at*.

a She gets up .... six o'clock .... the morning.

b I usually play football .... Sunday mornings.

c He always calls me .... midnight .... my birthday.

4 Write sentences (1) with *have/has got* (2) with *there is/are*.

a not / any coffee / but / some cakes.

We ....

There ....

b this hotel / any single rooms?

.... any single rooms?

.... in this hotel?

5 What are the missing verbs?

I live in Bristol but I work in London. I .... home at 6.15 in

the morning, and I .... the 6.25 train, which ....

in London at 8.00. Then I .... the underground to

Piccadilly, and I usually .... to work about 8.45. So the

whole journey .... about two and a half hours.

Phrasebook

Write this conversation in your language.

Two tickets to London, please.

....

....

Single or return?

Return.

That's £76, please.

....

....

When does the train leave?

At 7.15. From platform 5.

....

....

Writing *Punctuation*

1 Look at these sentences.

We usually go to church on Sundays.
Does Mary speak French?
I just love Italy in the spring!

Notice how we use these *punctuation marks* to end a sentence:

. (full stop)   **?** (question mark)   **!** (exclamation mark)

Notice that we use capital letters:

– at the beginning of a sentence
– for names of people and places
– for days and months
– for languages
– with the word *I*

2 Look at these words. Which ones should have capital letters?

ernest hemingway	october	london	the mountains
german	the alps	a language school	can i go now?
village	summer	tuesday	the oxford school of english
today			

3 Each sentence has *two* mistakes. Correct them.

a he speaks german but not Italian. ....

b Does this Train go to Moscow ....

c The meeting will be on friday 14th May ....

d can i get there by bus? ....

4 This paragraph should contain *eight* sentences. Rewrite it, adding punctuation and capital letters.

my sister has got a new bike and she spends nearly all her time on it every afternoon she comes home from school and quickly has something to eat then she goes out on her bike and cycles round the streets until it gets dark i never see her at weekends because she spends all day riding her bike in the evenings she reads magazines about cycling it's her birthday next week do you know what i'm going to give her i'm going to give her a mirror for her bike

5 Talking about now

A Verb + -ing

stand (+ ing)	→	standing
write (ǝ + ing)	→	writing
sit (+ t + ing)	→	sitting

Complete the crossword. All the answers end in *-ing*.

▶ ACROSS CLUES

2 – Where are you .... ?
– To the beach. Do you want to come? (5)

4 They're .... at the Royal Hotel. (7)

7 I'm .... some sandwiches for the children's lunch. (6)

9 He's on the phone. He's .... to his sister. (7)

11 He's putting on his clothes = he's .... dressed. (7)

14 She's .... her bike in the park. (6)

15 Are you .... a good time? (6)

16 – Why is that man .... ?
– He's trying to catch the bus. (7)

▼ DOWN CLUES

1 He can't come out. He's .... his homework. (5)

3 She's not feeling well. She's .... on the bed. (5)

5 Is he .... the children to school in the car? (6)

6 That boy's .... a cigarette. (7)

8 They're standing at the bus stop. They're .... for a bus. (7)

10 She's .... a book in the living room. (7)

12 He's in the bathroom. He's .... his hair. (7)

13 Slow down! You're .... too fast! (7)

Here's a list of all the verbs in the answers:
do, drive, get, go, have, lie, make, read, ride, run, smoke, stay, take, talk, wait, wash

B There's a woman playing the piano

Imagine you're on the phone at this party. Say what you can see, using *There is/are + -ing*.

1 (play)   There's a woman playing the piano.

2 (eat)   There are some people eating in the kitchen.

3 (dance)   ....

4 (read)   ....

5 (sing)   ....

6 (sit)   ....

7 (swim)   ....

C What's life like?

What's life like for these people at the moment? What do you think they're doing (and not doing)?
Here are some ideas (but you can use your own ideas, too).

see friends   read …   go out   study   watch TV   eat out   go to bed late   work hard   play …

1 We've got some friends staying with us at the moment. _We're eating out quite a lot._
We're also going out a lot in the evenings, so we're not watching much TV.
And we're _____

2 I've got three big examinations next week. _____

3 Helena's ill in bed. She's got 'flu. _____

Listening: *We're busy*

You will hear two people saying what they are doing
these days. Listen and complete the table. Write ✓ or ✗.

Is she/he	Woman	Man
1 very busy?		
2 studying for an exam?		
3 getting ready for visitors?		
4 reading a novel?		
5 moving mattresses?		
6 looking after a sick child?		
7 looking for a new house?		
8 looking for a job?		

Words

Write these words in your language.

travel (v.) _____

lie (v.) _____

climb _____

grass _____

chemistry _____

art college _____

garage _____

keep in touch _____

have a good time _____

earn _____

Other words

_____   _____

_____   _____

_____   _____

_____   _____

6 Food and drink

A Ingredients

N	O	O	D	L	E	S	B	P
A	L	A	M	B	B	U	E	R
U	S	A	U	S	A	G	E	A
B	P	R	S	P	G	E	F	W
E	A	C	H	I	C	K	E	N
R	G	A	R	C	P	O	R	K
G	H	R	O	E	R	N	S	P
I	E	R	O	S	R	I	C	E
N	T	O	M	A	T	O	A	P
E	T	T	S	N	D	N	C	P
H	I	S	C	H	E	E	S	E
G	A	R	L	I	C	I	P	R
S	P	O	T	A	T	O	E	S

There are 19 kinds of food in the wordsquare.
They are all ingredients in the dishes in Exercise 6.1.

15 of the letters are not used. Write them in the squares below, and you'll find something else to eat.

[ ][ ][ ][ ][ ][ ][ ] [ ][ ][ ] [ ][ ][ ][ ][ ]

B A healthy eater?

How often do you eat or drink the things in the list? Write four short paragraphs.

1 (every day) ....
....

2 (quite often) ....
....

3 (not very often) ....
....

4 (never) ....
....

| FRUIT |
| VEGETABLES |
| MEAT |
| FISH |
| CAKES & SWEETS |
| FAST FOOD |
| TEA & COFFEE |
| ALCOHOLIC DRINKS |
| OTHER DRINKS |

Are you a healthy eater? Give yourself a mark out of ten: ..../10..........

C A packet of biscuits

What food and drink can you see? What containers are they in? Write phrases.

1 ....
2 ....
3 ....
4 ....
5 ....
6 *a can of tomatoes*
7 ....
8 ....
9 *a bag of sweets*
10 ....

Listening: *Polish dishes*

🔲 A Polish woman talks about two typical dishes from Poland: *bigos* and *chlodnik*. Listen and answer the questions.

1 Which ingredients are for *bigos*? Which are for *chlodnik*? (Write *B* or *C*.)

| C | beetroot | ☐ | eggs | ☐ | meat |

☐ tomatoes   ☐ cream   ☐ bacon

☐ cabbage   ☐ spices   ☐ beetroot leaves

2 Which dish

a is a kind of soup? ....

b is usually eaten cold? ....

c tastes better the next day? ....

d is good to eat in summer? ....

Words

Write these words in your language.

piece (of meat) ....

kind (of meat) ....

stew ....

vegetables ....

fruit ....

How often ...? ....

healthy (food) ....

shopkeeper ....

shopping list ....

Other words

....

....

....

....

....

....

....

....

Check your progress

1 Write about the boy, using *love*, *hate*, *like* and *mind*.

a *He loves* ....

b ....

c ....

d ....

e ....

2 Simple or continuous? Put the verbs in the correct form.

In my family, we (*usually eat*) .... a lot of meat,

and we (*not eat*) .... much fruit. At the

moment, my cousin George (*stay*) .... with us.

He's a vegetarian – he (*not eat*) .... meat, and

he (*eat*) .... a lot of fruit. So just at the moment

we (*not eat*) .... any meat, and we (*eat*)

.... a lot of fruit.

3 Fill the gaps with expressions with *get*.

get in .... the bath → have a bath → .... the bath

.... the bus → travel → .... the bus

wake up → .... → have breakfast

4 What's in the picture? Say two things about each person.

There's a woman sitting ....

....

There's a boy ....

....

There's a girl ....

....

Phrasebook

Write these remarks in your language.

Let's sit here.

Could we see the menu, please?

What would you like?

I'd like a mushroom pizza, please.

Could we have the bill, please?

Writing *Reference*

1 Look at the examples. What do the words in *italics* refer to?

a Julia is my flat-mate, but I don't like *her* very much. *She* just watches TV all the time.

She/her   =   Julia ....

b Be careful with those eggs! Don't drop *them*, or *they* will break.

them/they   = ...

c A man went into the house. *He* stayed *there* for half an hour. Then *he* came out and got into a black car.

He/he   = ...

there   = ...

d – Do you like Rome?
  – Yes, I think *it's* a beautiful city. I often go *there* on business.

it   = ...

there   = ...

2 Fill each gap with a word from the list.

a – Do you know London?

  – Yes, I know .... very well. I live .... !

b My sister has a new flat. .... isn't very big, but .... likes ....

c My brother never writes to me. I write to .... every month, but .... never replies.

d – Where are the children? Can you see .... ?

  – Yes. I can see ....'re swimming in the river.

e – Does Paula still work in that café?

  – I don't think so. I was .... yesterday, and I didn't see ....

3 What's wrong with this story? Rewrite it using words from the list.

A new restaurant opened in town last week, so I went to the restaurant to see what the restaurant was like. A waitress came to my table and gave me a menu, but the waitress wasn't very friendly. I ordered chicken and chips. Half an hour later, the waitress brought the food. The food wasn't very good. The chicken was tough, and the chicken had a rather strange taste. The chips were cold and greasy. I couldn't eat the chips at all.

I called the waitress and asked the waitress to bring me the bill. The bill came to £25. I asked to see the manager. I told the manager that I thought £25 was too much for such a bad meal. I gave the manager £5 and then walked out of the restaurant. I'll never go to the restaurant again.

....
....
....
....
....
....
....
....
....
....
....
....
....
....
....
....
....

7 The past

A Irregular verbs

All the answers are in the Past simple tense. They are all irregular verbs.

> *Here's a list of the verbs used in the answers:*
>
> be, buy, drink, feel, give, go, have, leave, make, ride, send, sleep, swim, teach, throw, wake, wear, write
>
> *There's a list of irregular verbs on page 95.*

1 ▼ She jumped into the sea and
.... to the island. (4)

2 ▶ In the 1970s, computers
.... very expensive. (4)

3 ▼ He .... his bicycle to
the shops. (4)

4 ▶ I .... some sandwiches for
the children's lunch. (4)

1 ▶ Yesterday the weather ....
very cold. (3)

1 ▼ I .... them a letter. (5)

2 ▼ He .... for eight hours last
night. (5)

3 ▶ I .... up at 7.00 this
morning. (4)

4 ▶ I .... home at 8.00 and
arrived at the station at 8.30. (4)

1 ▶ He .... the ball
over the wall. (5)

2 ▼ I .... a shower this
morning. (3)

3 ▼ We .... to the cinema
last night. (4)

4 ▶ After the race, he .... two litres of water. (5)

1 ▼ She .... a new car
six months ago. (6)

2 ▼ I .... him several
emails, but he didn't
reply. (4)

3 ▶ I .... a suit at
the wedding. (4)

4 ▼ She .... him £50
for his birthday. (4)

5 ▶ My grandfather was a teacher. He .... music
and history. (6)

6 ▶ After the race, he .... very tired. (4)

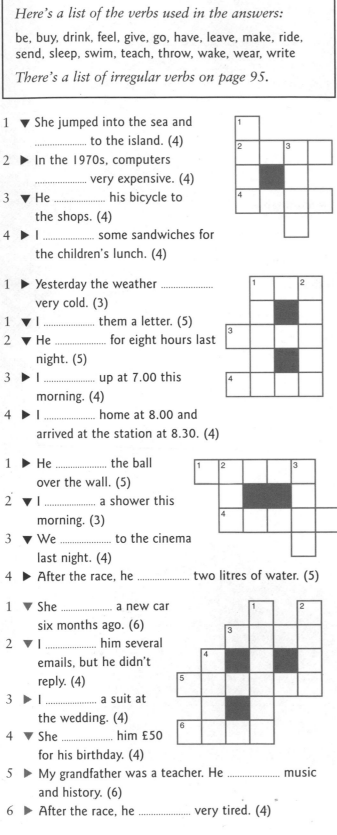

B Positive and negative

Bella and her husband Dick never do the same things on the same day. For example, yesterday

Bella *listened* to the radio.
Dick *didn't listen* to the radio.

What else happened (or didn't happen) yesterday?

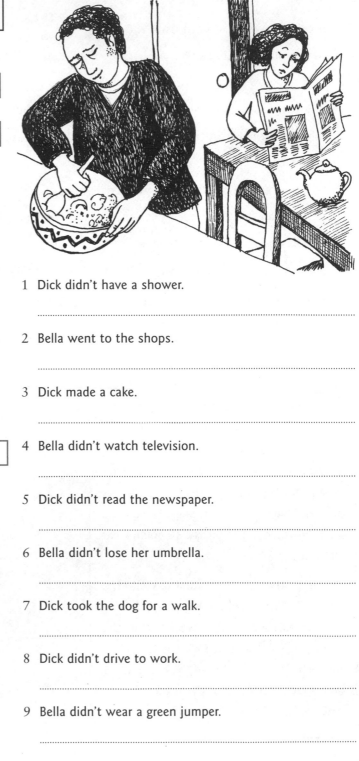

1 Dick didn't have a shower.

....

2 Bella went to the shops.

....

3 Dick made a cake.

....

4 Bella didn't watch television.

....

5 Dick didn't read the newspaper.

....

6 Bella didn't lose her umbrella.

....

7 Dick took the dog for a walk.

....

8 Dick didn't drive to work.

....

9 Bella didn't wear a green jumper.

....

C Asking Wh- questions

Rewrite these questions using question words from the box.

What
When
Why
Who
How
How much
Where

1 Did you invite John to dinner? Jane? Alice?

  Who did you invite to dinner?

2 Did they go to a restaurant last night? a theatre? a cinema?

  ....

3 Did he leave because he was tired? because he was ill? because he was bored?

  ....

4 Did you spend £50? £100? £500?

  ....

5 Did she say 'Hello'? 'Go away'? 'Goodbye'?

  ....

6 Did your mother arrive yesterday? two days ago? last week?

  ....

7 Did you get in with a key? by ringing the bell? by breaking a window?

  ....

Listening: *A man and a penguin*

1 🔲 Listen to this joke and put the pictures in order.

2 Listen again and fill the gaps.

A man found a penguin (a) ....

He took the penguin to (b) .... The

policeman told him to (c) ....

That evening, the policeman saw (d) ....

.... The policeman

said, 'I told you to (e) ....'

The man said, 'I took him (f) ....

Now (g) ....'

Words

Write these words in your language.

sandwich ....

(2 hours) later ....

several ....

customer ....

thick ....

thin ....

slice ....

delicious ....

gas ....

traffic light ....

unfortunately ....

Other words

....

....

....

....

8 A place to live

A Phrases

Complete these sentences with a suitable phrase. For each phrase use one item from Box A and one from Box B.

A	B
a main	~~centre~~
a view	floor
block	north
faces	of flats
looks out	of the sea
~~the city~~	on a park
the ninth	road

1 The trouble with living in .... *the city centre* .... is that you can never find a place to park your car.

2 They live on the coast. Their living room window has ....

3 Our bedroom window .... , so it doesn't get much sun.

4 A lot of cars, buses and lorries go past our house: we live on ....

5 Our balcony .... – it's a very pleasant place to sit.

6 I live right at the top of a tall ....

7 I hope the lift is working: he lives on .... !

B What are they like?

Find adjectives in the box which could describe

clean	quiet
convenient	~~small~~
dark	spacious
dirty	sunny
light	tidy
noisy	untidy

1 a flat with one room   *small*

2 a house near a busy airport   ....

3 a house on a hillside facing south   ....

4 a room with a lot of things lying on the floor   ....

5 a flat near the shops and schools   ....

6 a house with very small windows   ....

7 a house in a street with very little traffic   ....

8 a house with large rooms   ....

9 the room in the picture   ....

Write one or two sentences about your house or flat. Use adjectives from the box.

I live in ....

It's ....

C Things in rooms

Look at rooms A–D. What kind of rooms are they?

What is there in each room? Where in the room?
Complete these sentences.

1 There's a suitcase *under the bed* .

2 .... above the bed.

3 There's a cupboard ....

4 .... by the door.

5 There are some jars ....

6 .... between the cooker
and the sink.

7 There's a washbasin ....

8 .... on the floor.

9 There's a mirror ....

10 .... on the sofa.

11 There's a lamp ....

12 .... on the television.

A *bedroom* .... B ....

C .... D ....

Listening: *Favourite rooms*

Two people talk about their favourite room. For each
room, find *five* differences from the sentences below.

1

> My favourite room is in the cellar. It's a small room, with
> two chairs, a shelf full of old books, a stereo and two
> small speakers. I often sit down there and read.

a ....

b ....

c ....

d ....

e ....

2

> My daughter's bedroom is quite big. It's rather dark,
> but it's warm and comfortable. It has a metal bed, a
> wooden cupboard, and a shelf which runs round the
> room and has books on it. There's a chair by the door.

a ....

b ....

c ....

d ....

e ....

Words

Write these words in your language.

fairly ....

the suburbs ....

lovely ....

position ....

on the edge of ....

square (n.) ....

recently ....

in the middle ....

suitcase ....

Other words

....

....

....

....

D Study pages

Check your progress

1 Write sentences about the two men.

a Both ....

....

b Neither .... hair.

c One ....

the other ....

2 It is now the afternoon of Friday 15 September. Here are some parts of a man's diary.

Wed 13 Sept: Mum and Dad	Sat 9 Sept: Party 9.00 p.m.
Sat 15 March: To USA	Fri 15 Sept: Doctor, 10.00 a.m.
Thurs 14 Sept: Cinema 3.00 p.m.	

Now complete these sentences with a past time expression.

a He went to the cinema *yesterday afternoon.* ....

b He went to a party ....

c He saw the doctor ....

d He went the USA ....

e He saw his parents ....

3 Complete the conversation. Use the Past simple tense.

A .... last month.   (I/go/London)

B Really? .... a good time?   (you/have)

A Yes, ... very interesting.   (it/be)

B ....? In a hotel? (where/you/stay)

A No, ... in a friend's flat.   (I/stay)

B And ....?   (what/you/do)

A Well, ... me to Buckingham   (friend/take)

Palace, but .... the Queen.   (we/not/see)

4 Read the descriptions, and write one word in each gap.

a He lives in a big .... of flats. His flat's on the fifth

.... , and it .... out over the city centre.

b I live on a busy .... road, so my flat's quite .... ,

but it's very .... for the shops.

c Her living Room .... south, and has big windows, so

it's very .... , and there's a lovely .... of the

mountains.

Phrasebook

Write this conversation in your language.

....

....

....

....

....

....

....

....

....

Writing *Joining ideas*

1 Look at these examples.

His flat is on the third floor. It's got a balcony.
His flat is on the third floor **and** it's got a balcony.

Their house is very big. It's only got a small garden.
Their house is very big **but** it's only got a small garden.

My flat is on a main road. It's rather noisy.
My flat is on a main road **so** it's rather noisy.

2 Fill the gaps with *and*, *but* or *so*.

a Our flat is very old .... it's in good condition.

b My flat is near the town centre .... it's very convenient for the shops.

c Her cottage is very comfortable .... it's rather damp in winter.

d He lives near an underground station .... it doesn't take long to get into the centre.

e My flat faces south .... it has a big balcony.

3 Paragraphs A and B say the same thing, but one paragraph presents the ideas in a more natural way. Which one?

A I'm quite pleased with my new flat. It has three bedrooms and a large kitchen. It's near the city centre, so it's very convenient for my work. Unfortunately, it's on the ground floor, so it's a bit dark.

B I'm quite pleased with my new flat. It has a large kitchen. It's near the city centre and it has three bedrooms. Unfortunately, it's on the ground floor, so it's a bit dark. It's very convenient for my work.

4 Join these ideas together to make a paragraph. Use *and*, *but* or *so* where necessary.

It's not too noisy.

It has a living room, a bedroom and a small kitchen.

It has a beautiful view of the sea.

It's near the town centre.

It's near the beach.

I've got a new flat.

It's a long way from the main road.

9 I've done it!

A What's the rule?

Write the correct forms of the verbs in the puzzle.

1 He isn't asleep. He has just (OPEN) his eyes.
2 My hands are clean. I've just (WASH) them.
3 Have you (SELL) your car yet?
4 They've just (GET) into the lift.
5 He's just (PUT) on his coat.
6 I haven't (HAVE) my breakfast yet.
7 Oh dear. I think I've (BREAK) my arm!
8 Have you (BUY) me a present?
9 She has (WRITE) three postcards.
10 Ouch! I've (CUT) my finger!
11 The train has (ARRIVE) at the station.
12 I've just (SPEAK) to her on the phone.
13 They haven't (LEAVE) the house yet.
14 The children have (GO) home.

> *There's a list of irregular verbs on page 95.*

Now complete this rule:

Present perfect tense = have *or* has + ...

B I'm ready!

What have these people done? Write about them using the Present perfect tense. Use ideas from the list. If you like, you can add your own ideas.

buy / ticket	cook / meal	put on / music
clean / teeth	find / passport	pack / case
clean / house	get into bed	say 'Goodnight'

1 Some friends are coming for dinner tonight. Jack and Sylvia are all ready …
They've cleaned the house. They've
....
....

2 Maria's going on a trip to the USA. She's ready to leave …
....
....
....

3 It's nine o'clock. The children are ready to go to sleep …
....
....
....

C Positive and negative

What have these people done? What haven't they done? Write two sentences for each situation.

1
have a bath
have a shower

2
paint a picture
take a photo

3
get married
get divorced

4
drink his lemonade
eat his sandwich

5
win the game
lose the game

1 *He hasn't had a bath. He's had a shower.*

2 ....

3 ....

4 ....

5 ....

Listening: *What has happened?*

 Listen to the four conversations and match them with the pictures.

A

B

C

D

Answer these questions.

Conversation 1
a What's the problem?
b Where are the glasses?

Conversation 2
a What has happened?
b How did they meet?

Conversation 3
a What has she done?
b What does she do now?

Conversation 4
a What has happened?
b How did it happen?

Words

Write these words in your language.

break (a leg) ....

put on (a coat) ....

get on (a bus) ....

get off (a bus) ....

get into (a lift) ....

turn on (a light) ....

turn off (a light) ....

pack (a case) ....

hairdresser ....

Other words

....

....

....

....

....

....

10 Clothes

A What are they wearing?

What are these people wearing? Write sentences.

1 _She's wearing a blouse, earrings,_
....

2 ....
....

3 ....
....

4 ....
....

5 ....
....

6 ....
....

B Buying clothes

Here's a conversation from the Classroom Book unit. Can you unscramble the sentences in *italics*?

1 _What size is this coat?_ ....

2 ....

3 ....

4 ....

5 ....

6 ....

7 ....

8 ....

9 ....

10 ....

Customer	Excuse me. (1) *Size what coat this is?*
Assistant	It's 46.
Customer	Oh, good. (2) *On can it I try?*
Assistant	Yes, of course. (3) *Are here you.*
Customer	Thanks. (4) *Look does how it?*
Assistant	Mmm. (5) *Very looks good it.* (6) *You suits really it.* (7) *OK it feel does?*
Customer	Yes, it's fine. (8) *Well fits it very.* It's really comfortable. (9) *It how is much?*
Assistant	It's £65.
Customer	OK. (10) *Not expensive too that's.* I think I'll buy it.

C When do you wear …?

Read about this person. Are you the same? Choose
five of these things and say when you wear them.

| a tie | boots | sandals | gloves | jeans |
| make-up | a hat | shorts | trainers | glasses |

1 ....

....

2 ....

....

3 ....

....

4 ....

....

5 ....

....

I never wear a tie.

I always wear make-up when I go out.

I wear a hat when it's cold – and when it's sunny.

I only wear gloves when I'm washing dishes.

I usually wear shorts and trainers when I go running.

I wear glasses for driving and for watching television.

I don't wear jeans very often during the week, but I sometimes wear them at the weekend.

Listening: *Working clothes*

1 ▭ **Three people say what they wear to work. Listen and complete the table.**

	Which picture?	What clothes?
1		
2		
3		

A   B   C

2 **What do you know about the three people's jobs?**

Speaker 1 ....

Speaker 2 ....

Speaker 3 ....

Words

Write these words in your language.

cotton ....

denim ....

leather ....

pair (of socks) ....

smart (clothes) ....

fit (v.) ....

It's fine ....

special occasion ....

business ....

Other words

....

....

....

....

....

....

Check your progress

1 Replace the phrases in *italics* with possessive pronouns.

a – Whose coat is this? Is it ....*yours*........ (*your coat*)?

– No. .... (*My coat*) is green. Perhaps it's

.... (*Alan's coat*).

b – Which is better, our car or .... (*their car*)?

– .... (*Our car*). It's cheaper to run.

2 Choose the Present perfect or the Past simple.

a Look. *I've written / I wrote* three letters. *I've written / I wrote* three yesterday, too.

b *Have you gone / Did you go* to the beach last weekend?

c – *Has he woken up / Did he wake up* yet?

– Yes. *He's woken up / He woke up* an hour ago.

d Sorry. She's not here. *She hasn't come / She didn't come* home from work yet.

3 What does the *'s* mean?

a Mary's arrived ....

b Mary's car ....

c Mary's here ....

4 Complete the conversation. Use the Present perfect tense.

A I think we're ready. ....*I've*.................... my case, (I/pack)

and .... our passports. (I/find)

.... your case? (you/pack)

B Yes. But .... my hair. (I/not/wash)

A What about Sara? ....? (she/phone)

B Yes, she has. .... the tickets (she/buy)

but .... them yet. (she/not/collect)

A Hmm. So maybe we're not ready, after all.

5 Write three ...

a ... things people wear to go running

....

b ... things people wear to go skiing

....

c ... kinds of jewellery

....

Phrasebook

Write this conversation in your language.

Can I pay by cheque?

I'm sorry. We don't take cheques.

....

....

Well, do you take credit cards?

Yes, credit cards are fine.

....

....

Could I have a receipt, please?

....

Writing *Sequence (1)*

My next-door neighbour has a regular daily routine. He always leaves home at exactly nine in the morning. First he goes to the newsagent's and buys the morning paper. Then he goes to a café (always the same one), orders a cup of black coffee and reads his paper. After that he goes for a walk once round the park, and then he goes home.

1 These expressions are used for showing sequence. Find them in the text.

| then |
| and then |
| after that |
| and |
| first |

Which are used

a to begin a new sentence? ....

b to join sentences together? ....

2 Join these sentences together to complete the paragraph. Use expressions from the box.

I collect the children from school.

I take them to the park.

We come home.

We have supper together.

I play with them for an hour.

They have a bath.

They get ready for bed.

I tell them a story.

I can sit down and relax.

Don't ever try to phone me between three o'clock and seven o'clock, because I'm always busy.

3 Are there any times in your day when you have a regular routine? Write about them.

11 Quantity

A A, some and any

Fill the gaps in these stories with *a(n)*, *some* or *any*.

Spaghetti

Yesterday I wanted spaghetti bolognese for dinner. I bought
(1) .... meat at the butcher, and got (2) ....
tomatoes at the supermarket. Then I remembered that I didn't
have (3) .... cheese, so I bought (4) .... nice big piece, and went home – and found that there wasn't
(5) .... spaghetti. So I had (6) .... cheese sandwich instead.

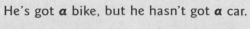

He's got *a* bike, but he hasn't got *a* car.

We drank **some** lemonade, and we ate **some** sweets.

Have you got **any** money? There isn't **any** food. And I haven't got **any** cigarettes.

Elephants

I was on a train in Germany, and I saw (7) .... man with
(8) .... large packet of flour standing by (9) ....
open window. As I watched, he took (10) .... flour and
threw it out of the window. Then he threw (11) .... more.

'Why are you doing that?' I asked.

'To keep the elephants away,' he replied.

'But there aren't (12) .... elephants in Germany,' I said.

'You see,' he said, 'it works!'

B Quantity expressions

The sentences below aren't true. Rewrite them with different quantity expressions.

1 There are *very few* polar bears in Antarctica.
   There aren't any polar bears in Antartica.

2 There are *quite a lot of* people in Antarctica.
   ....

3 There are *hardly any* cars in Los Angeles.
   ....

4 Nurses earn *plenty of* money.
   ....

5 There's *a lot of* rain in the Sahara Desert.
   ....

6 *Not many* people speak Spanish.
   ....

7 Bill Gates has got *very little* money.
   ....

8 There are *lots of* colour photos in this book.
   ....

a lot of
lots of
plenty of

quite a lot of

not many/much

very few/little
hardly any

not any

C Too and enough

There are too many advertisements.

There's too much pop music.

There aren't enough good programmes.

They don't show enough sport.

What are these people thinking? Complete the sentences, using *too much*, *too many* or *not enough*.

1 .... work.

2 .... time.

3 .... holidays.

4 .... money.

5 .... young people.

6 .... old people.

7 .... things to do.

Listening: *A healthy diet*

1 🔲 You will hear two people saying what food they eat. Give each speaker a score out of 5 for each type of food (5 = a lot, 0 = none).

	Speaker 1	Speaker 2
sweet things		
fat		
vegetables		
fruit		
meat		
fish		

2 Which person has a healthier diet?

....

Words

Write these words in your language.

mouse ....

parrot ....

jewellery ....

gold ....

in fact ....

fresh fruit ....

fresh air ....

rubbish ....

traffic ....

crime ....

complaint ....

Other words

....

....

....

....

12 How do you feel?

A Where does it hurt?

These people all have aches and pains. Where does it hurt?
Write your answers in the puzzle.

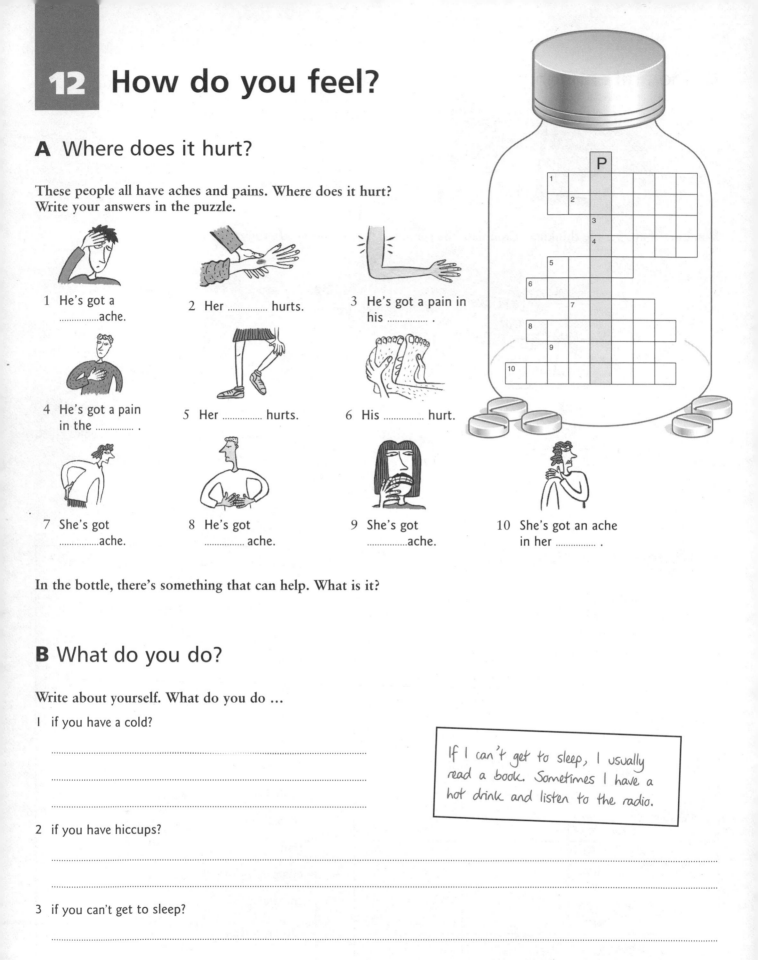

1 He's got a
..............ache.

2 Her .... hurts.

3 He's got a pain in
his ....

4 He's got a pain
in the ....

5 Her .... hurts.

6 His .... hurt.

7 She's got
..............ache.

8 He's got
.... ache.

9 She's got
..............ache.

10 She's got an ache
in her ....

In the bottle, there's something that can help. What is it?

B What do you do?

Write about yourself. What do you do …

1 if you have a cold?

....

....

....

If I can't get to sleep, I usually
read a book. Sometimes I have a
hot drink and listen to the radio.

2 if you have hiccups?

....

....

3 if you can't get to sleep?

....

....

4 if you have 'flu?

....

....

C The right medicine

Fill each gap in the story with one word.

Yesterday lunchtime, I got a nasty (1) ....

in my stomach. I took two (2) .... , but

I still (3) .... ill, so I made an

(4) .... to see the doctor. The doctor

(5) .... my stomach. Then he smiled and

wrote a (6) .... for some medicine. On the

way home, I stopped at the (7) .... to get

my medicine, but the assistant just laughed, and said 'You're in

the wrong place.' And she gave me back the (8) ....

I read it. It said 'There's nothing wrong with your stomach. But

your (9) .... are too small. Go to a clothes shop and buy a bigger pair.'

Listening: *Ouch!*

1 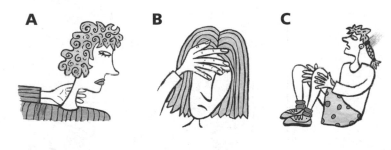 Listen to the conversations and match them with the pictures. What is each person's problem?

A **B** **C**

....

....

2 Which conversation is each sentence about?
Write *1*, *2* or *3*.

a ☐ She went to a party.

b ☐ She slipped and fell over.

c ☐ She doesn't know how it happened.

d ☐ She can't stand up.

e ☐ She decided to lie down.

f ☐ It started when she woke up this morning.

g ☐ She thinks she has broken something.

h ☐ She doesn't like cigarette smoke.

i ☐ She can't drive her car.

Words

Write these words in your language.

What's the matter? ....

heavy ....

broom ....

brandy ....

'flu ....

hiccups ....

feel sick ....

dentist ....

count (v.) ....

aspirin ....

Other words

....

....

....

....

....

Check your progress

1 Write about Ed and Laura using *for* and *since*.

> Ed was born in 1965, and moved to London in 1980. He left school in 1982 and started working for Barclays Bank, where he still works. He and his wife Laura got married in 1990. For several years they rented a flat, but five years ago they bought a house, and just six months ago they bought a computer.

a Ed has lived .... 1980.

b He .... 1982.

c Ed and Laura .... 1990.

d They .... five years.

e They .... six months.

2 Choose the correct words.

a I've got ☐ some / ☐ any sugar, but I haven't got ☐ some / ☐ any milk.

b ☐ There's / ☐ There are ☐ too much / ☐ too many cars in this town, and ☐ there's / ☐ there are ☐ too much / ☐ too many noise.

c He's got ☐ very few / ☐ very little friends and ☐ very few / ☐ very little money.

3 Fill the gaps with one word.

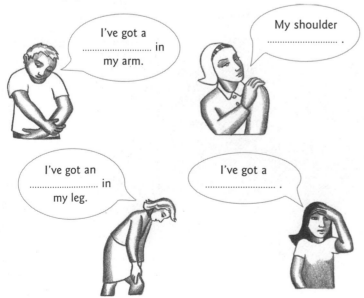

I've got a .... in my arm.

My shoulder ....

I've got an .... in my leg.

I've got a ....

Phrasebook

Write these expressions in your language.

Hello. I'd like to make an appointment to see a doctor.

....

....

Is it urgent?

Fairly urgent, yes.

....

....

OK. Can you come this morning?

Yes I can.

....

....

How about 10.30?

Yes, that's fine.

....

....

Writing *Lists*

1 Look at these sentences:

> Eva was really ill.
> 1   She had a headache.
> 2   She felt sick.
> 3   She couldn't sleep.

We can join the ideas together like this:

a   Eva was really ill. She had a headache, she felt sick and she couldn't sleep.

b   Eva was really ill. She had a headache and she felt sick. Also, she couldn't sleep.

2 Punctuate these sentences.

a   I really enjoyed the party the food was delicious there was lots of good music and I met some very interesting people.

....

....

....

....

b   I don't like my flat-mate much she never cleans the flat and she plays loud music all the time also she has some very strange friends.

....

....

....

....

3 Add some ideas to these sentences. Use expressions from the box.

a   I don't like going into the city centre on Saturdays. ....

....

....

b   That dress looks really good on you. ....

....

....

c   After 20 miles, she knew she couldn't walk any further. ....

....

....

d   It's a very good restaurant. ....

....

....

It's very clean
There's nowhere to park
It's a very unusual colour
The food's always freshly cooked
Her legs ached
The shops are very crowded
She felt tired and hungry
It goes with your eyes
The streets are full of traffic
It's not too expensive
It's just the right length
Her feet hurt

13 What will happen?

A Will and won't

Make two predictions about each person, one with *will* and one with *won't*. Use the verbs in the box.

catch	fail	~~forget~~	go	lose	miss	pass	remember	stay	win

1 Tom has a terrible memory. It's his sister's birthday next week.

He'll forget his sister's birthday.   He won't

2 Maria's exams are tomorrow. She hasn't done any work.

3 Ed's bus goes at 8.30. It's 8.25 and he's just woken up.

4 Alan's learning to play tennis. He's got a match against the number 1 player in his school.

5 Natasha has tickets for a concert this evening. She has 'flu.

B Questions with 'will'

Ask questions with *will*. Some are *Yes/no* questions, and some are *Wh-* questions.

1 Spartak Moscow might win tonight, or they might not.

Will Spartak Moscow win tonight?

2 We might need three chickens. Or four. Or five …

How many chickens will we need?

3 The train might arrive at 2.00. Or 2.30. Or 3.00 …

4 It might be windy tomorrow, or it might not.

5 There might be food at the party, or there might not.

6 You might be at home tomorrow afternoon. Or at work. Or at the cinema …

7 I might see you again tomorrow. Or next week. Or next year …

8 She might pass her exam, or she might not.

9 The tickets might cost £20. Or £25. Or £30 …

C The next three years

What do you think will happen in your life in the next three years? Make some predictions from the table.

....

....

....

....

....

....

....

....

	go abroad.
	change jobs.
	write a novel.
	leave school.
I'll	get married.
I'll probably	win lots of money.
I might	start smoking.
I probably won't	stop smoking.
I won't	learn another language.
	have a baby.
	move house.
	buy a car.
	appear on TV.

Now make three predictions of your own.

I'll probably ....

I might ....

I probably won't ....

Listening: *Giving blood*

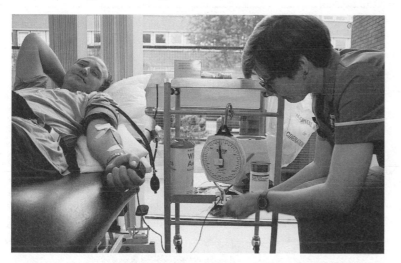

You're planning to give blood, and someone is telling you what will happen. Before you listen, check that you know these words and phrases:

a nurse	take a sample of your blood
a needle	your blood group

🔊 **Now listen. What are the answers to these questions?**

1 What will I have to do? ....

2 How much blood will they take? ....

3 Will it hurt? ....

4 How long will it take? ....

5 How will I feel afterwards? ....

Words

Write these words in your language.

stranger	....
special	....
important	....
forget	....
swimsuit	....
war	....
peace	....
energy	....
disease	....
attack	....

Other words

....	....
....	....
....	....
....	....
....	....

14 About town

A Places to go (1)

There are 19 places to go in the wordsquare.
Can you find

1 three places to eat and drink?
café

2 three religious places?
church

3 two places to dance (until late)?

4 two places to see exhibitions?

5 a place to see animals?

6 three places where you sit in the audience?

7 a place like the one in the picture?

8 four places for exercise and sport?

S	W	I	M	M	I	N	G	P	O	O	L
P	N	M	O	S	Q	U	E	C	W	X	C
O	I	U	P	A	R	K	D	I	S	C	O
R	G	S	C	A	F	E	C	N	S	C	N
T	H	E	A	T	R	E	A	E	T	H	C
S	T	U	S			T	M	A	U	E
C	C	M	T			H	A	D	R	R
E	L	B	L			E	Z	I	C	T
N	U	A	E			D	O	U	H	H
T	B	R	Q			R	O	M	Z	A
R	E	S	T	A	U	R	A	N	T	P	L
E	A	R	T	G	A	L	L	E	R	Y	L

B Places to go (2)

What places are there for visitors in your town? Think of three suitable places, and write one or two
sentences about each one.

1 a place to go sightseeing

Go and see the main square in the
old town. It's got a cathedral and
a lot of other old buildings.

2 a place to go shopping

Parade Street is a good place to go
shopping. The shops there have got
very good leather bags and jackets,
and you can get shoes, too.

3 a place to go for an evening out

The King's Theatre often has good
plays and musicals, and sometimes
they have concerts.

C Giving directions

Complete the conversations
using expressions from the box.

Example:

A Excuse me. Can you tell me the
way to the post office?

B Yes. You go straight along this
road. Go over the river, and then
turn right at the cinema. You'll
see it on the left.

Turn	left right	(at …)
Go straight on.		
Go	under over past	…
You'll see it It's	on the	left. right.

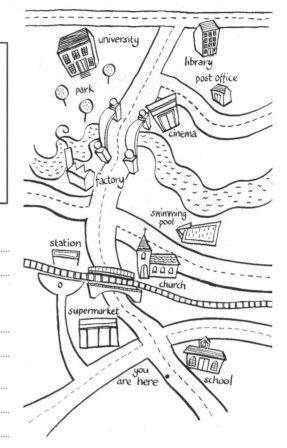

A Excuse me. How do I get to the university?

B ....

....

A Excuse me. Can you tell me the way to the swimming pool?

B ....

....

A Excuse me. ....

B ....

....

Listening: *Living in London*

You will hear a man and a woman talking about living
in London.

1 Which things does the man talk about? Which does the
woman talk about? Write *M* or *W*.

a ☐ going to work

b ☐ going out in the evening

c ☐ noise

d ☐ meeting people

e ☐ the atmosphere of the city

2 What do they say about each topic? Write a sentence for
each one.

a The underground is always full of people.

b ....

c ....

d ....

e ....

Words

Write these words in your language.

night life ....

see the sights ....

souvenir ....

culture ....

relax ....

atmosphere ....

postcard ....

a good selection ....

good quality ....

helpful ....

Other words

....

....

....

....

G Study pages

Check your progress

1 Do you remember this conversation? What are the sentences in *italics*?

A Don't forget to phone me.

B OK. (a) *I / phone / when / I / get / airport.*

A And send me a postcard. Don't forget.

B Yes. (b) *when / I / get / hotel / I / send / postcard.*

A And be careful.

B Don't worry. (c) *I / phone / if / anything / happen.*

A Well, (d) *if / you / not / phone / I / phone / hotel* – just to be sure …

a ....

b ....

c ....

d ....

2 Write two short answers, one positive and one negative.

a Does she speak English?   Yes, ...
   No, ...

b Have they left yet? ....
....

c Will it snow tomorrow? ....
....

3 Complete these predictions, using *will*, *won't*, *might* and *probably*.

a We ......will...... find a cure for cancer. (Yes!)

b I .... get 'flu this winter. (Yes, I think)

c There .... be another war. (I don't know)

d The world .... end tomorrow. (No, I think)

e We .... win the lottery this weekend. (No!)

4 Give directions from ✗ to the museum.

You go ....

....

....

....

....

....

....

(map showing school, cinema, museum)

Phrasebook

Write this conversation in your language.

Two tickets for Star Wars, please.

Both adults?

No, one adult and one child.

That's £13, please.

What time does the film start?

At 7.30.

Writing *Reason and contrast*

1 Look at these examples.

so *as* *because*	It's a very beautiful old city, **so** it's always full of tourists in summer. **As** **Because** it's a very beautiful old city, it's always full of tourists in summer.

but *although*	It's a very beautiful town to look at, **but** there isn't much to do there. **Although** it's a very beautiful town to look at, there isn't much to do there.

2 Fill the gaps with *so*, *as*, *because*, *but* or *although*.

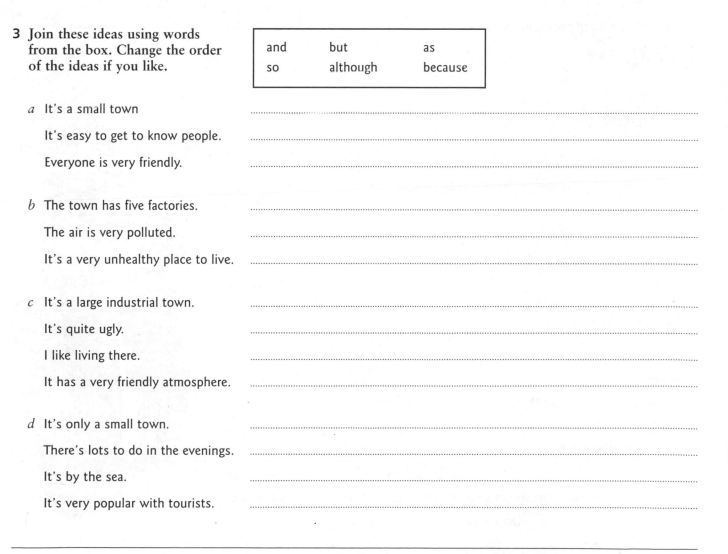

a .... there aren't any good restaurants, there are plenty of cheap cafés.

b .... it's a large sea port, it's full of people from all over the world, and there's always a lot going on.

c There's a large cinema, ... they don't show very interesting films .... I don't go there very often.

d The river's very polluted .... it's not a good idea to swim in it, ... there's a very good swimming pool.

3 Join these ideas using words from the box. Change the order of the ideas if you like.

and	but	as
so	although	because

a It's a small town

  It's easy to get to know people.

  Everyone is very friendly.

....

....

....

b The town has five factories.

  The air is very polluted.

  It's a very unhealthy place to live.

....

....

....

c It's a large industrial town.

  It's quite ugly.

  I like living there.

  It has a very friendly atmosphere.

....

....

....

....

d It's only a small town.

  There's lots to do in the evenings.

  It's by the sea.

  It's very popular with tourists.

....

....

....

....

15 Comparing things

A Yes, but …

Reply to these remarks. Use a comparative form.

1 – New York's a busy city, isn't it?
   – Yes, but _Tokyo's busier._

2 – I think dogs are very intelligent animals.
   – Yes, but _cats are more intelligent._

3 – Italy's a hot country, isn't it?
   – Yes, but ....

4 – I think English is a difficult language.
   – Yes, but ....

5 – Manchester United is a good football team.
   – Yes, but ....

6 – I think *Yesterday* is a beautiful song.
   – Yes, but ....

7 – Crocodiles are really ugly, aren't they?
   – Yes, but ....

8 – There are a lot of people in Russia.
   – Yes, but ....

Comparative and superlative forms
One-syllable adjectives cold – colder – coldest big – bigger – biggest
Two-syllable adjectives *ending in y:* friendly – friendlier – friendliest ugly – uglier – ugliest
most others: boring – more boring – most boring helpful – more helpful – most helpful
Three or more syllables popular – more popular – most popular expensive – more expensive – most expensive
Irregular adjectives good – better – best bad – worse – worst far – further – furthest much/many – more – most

B Opposites

Rewrite each sentence using an opposite adjective. Example:

Dogs are *smaller* than horses → Horses are *bigger* than dogs.

1 Gold is *more expensive* than silver.

   Silver ....

2 Schoolchildren are *younger* than university students.

   University students ....

3 Metal is *heavier* than plastic.

   Plastic ....

4 California is *wetter* than Arizona.

   Arizona ....

5 Listening is *more difficult* than reading.

   Reading ....

6 Africa is *poorer* than Europe.

   Europe ....

The first letters of the adjectives in answers 1–6 give the missing word below.

7 Mars is ☐☐☐☐☐☐ than Venus.

C World records

What world records can you find in the box? Some words are used more than once.

The Vatican		
China	high	population
Russia	small	mountain
The whale	large	river
The cheetah	fast	country
The Nile	long	animal
Everest		

1 *The Vatican is the smallest country in the world.* ....

2 *China has got* ....

3 ....

4 ....

5 ....

6 ....

7 ....

Listening: *The most and the fewest*

You will hear three people (A, B and C) talking about the languages they speak and the countries they have visited.

1 Which person

  a ☐ speaks the most languages?

  b ☐ speaks the fewest languages?

  c ☐ has visited the most countries?

  d ☐ has visited the fewest countries?

2 Which speakers have been to

  a ☐ Mexico?

  b ☐ Germany?

  c ☐ Japan?

3 Which speakers could understand people in

  a ☐ Mexico?

  b ☐ Germany?

  c ☐ Japan?

Words

Write these words in your language.

staff ....

helpful ....

reliable ....

lively ....

relaxing ....

attractive ....

spider ....

fly (n.) ....

consist of ....

Other words

....

....

....

....

....

16 Free time

A Things people do

What do you think these people do in their spare time? For each person, use two ideas from the list, and add one idea of your own.

I play	chess.	I often go	climbing.
	basketball.		cycling.
	the piano.		swimming.

I	like	(playing) chess.
	enjoy	(listening to) jazz.
		cycling.

Ed is only interested in sport.. *He plays golf, and he's quite a good table-tennis player. He also enjoys watching basketball, and often goes to watch his local team.*

Carol loves collecting things. ....

Jane's very musical. ....

Jim spends all his time reading. ....

Leo hates sport, but he likes playing games. ....

Flo's good at making things with her hands. ....

Bill enjoys outdoor activities. ....

- ☐ cards
- ☐ chess
- ☐ climb
- ☐ coins
- ☐ cycle
- ☑ golf
- ☐ jazz
- ☐ knit
- ☐ paint
- ☐ poetry
- ☐ science fiction
- ☐ shells
- ☑ table-tennis
- ☐ violin

Now write about yourself. What do you do in your spare time?

....

....

....

B Sports

Complete the crossword.

In MOTOR-RACING, you ⟨8⟩ a car round a ⟨2⟩, and in HORSE-RACING you ⟨3⟩ a horse round a ⟨2⟩. The person with the fastest time wins the ⟨1⟩.

If you want to play tennis, football, golf or basketball, you need a ⟨7⟩.

In TENNIS, there are two or four ⟨4►⟩. They ⟨14⟩ the ⟨7⟩ over the ⟨15⟩ with their ⟨13⟩.

In FOOTBALL, you ⟨11⟩ the ⟨7⟩ and try to score a ⟨9▼⟩.

In GOLF, you ⟨14⟩ the ⟨7⟩ with a ⟨6⟩ and try to knock it into the ⟨10⟩.

And in BASKETBALL, you ⟨12⟩ the ⟨7⟩, and if you can get it in the ⟨5⟩ you score ⟨4▼⟩. The team with the most ⟨4▼⟩ wins the ⟨9►⟩.

Listening: *Rock climbing*

You will hear a woman talking about rock climbing. Before you listen, find out what these words mean:

to concentrate	exciting	a steep slope
to bounce	frightened	a wall of rock
to slither		

1 Listen to the first part. Why does the woman like rock climbing? Choose *three* of these reasons.

a ☐ because it's exciting

b ☐ because it's difficult

c ☐ because it's dangerous

d ☐ because you have to think hard

e ☐ because it makes you forget your problems

2 Listen to the second part. Choose the picture that best matches what she says.

A  ☐

B  ☐

What is she thinking? Write two sentences to go in the bubble.

Words

Write these words in your language.

hobby ....

novel (n.) ....

decorate ....

skateboard ....

sailing ....

musical
instrument ....

hunting ....

frightened ....

be afraid
(of heights) ....

Other words

....

....

....

....

....

....

....

....

Check your progress

1 Rewrite these sentences using *good at* ...

a He can play the guitar very well.

He's very good at

b I can cook quite well.

c She can't speak French very well.

d They can't remember people's names at all.

2 Rewrite these sentences using *less* or *fewer*.

a Spiders have more legs than flies.

Flies

b Cars use more petrol than motorbikes.

Motorbikes

3 Fill the gaps with a suitable form of *go, go for* or *play*.

a Last weekend we .... a picnic in the mountains.

b Shall we .... swimming? Shall we .... a walk? Or shall we stay here and .... cards?

c He's very athletic. He .... climbing every weekend, and he .... skiing every winter.

d I enjoy .... basketball.

4 Complete these comparative and superlatives sentences.

a In the 60s, the Beatles were .... band in the world. (*popular*)

b Your parents are much .... than mine. (*friendly*)

c Last year's exam was quite easy, but this year it was much .... (*difficult*)

d Ben Nevis is .... mountain in Britain. (*high*)

Phrasebook

Write these conversations in your language.

Writing *Sequence (2)*

1 The words in the box below are used for showing sequence.
Find them in the two texts and underline them.

first
then
and
after (a few minutes)
(an hour) later

First we drove for a few miles along the main road, and then we turned down a narrow lane. Half an hour later we came to an old farmhouse.

We went into the football stadium and found our seats. After about ten minutes, the crowd started cheering and the two teams came onto the pitch. A few minutes later the match began.

2 Rewrite these sentences with correct punctuation.

a I first met him at a party in London about a year later I met him again

....

....

b She put the phone down after a few seconds she picked it up again and dialled a number

....

....

....

3 Fill the gaps with sequence expressions from the box.

a We bought a programme .... found our seats. .... the curtains opened .... the play began.

b A man went into the house .... closed the door. .... he came out again carrying a black box.

c .... I had a long, hot bath. .... I sat in bed .... read a book. .... I fell asleep.

4 Put this story in the correct order using sequence expressions.

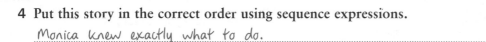

Monica knew exactly what to do.

....

....

....

....

....

....

....

....

....

Edward arrived home.
The taxi arrived.
Monica knew exactly what to do.
She called a taxi.
Monica closed the door and posted her keys through the letter box.
She packed a small suitcase.
She wrote a letter and put it on the table.
The letter said 'Goodbye, Edward. I've had enough.'

17 Rules and advice

A Children's questions

Imagine you're a child in these situations. Ask questions with *Can …?* and *Do … have to …?*

1 Your parents want to watch the news on TV, and there are cartoons on another channel.

Do we have to watch the news?

Can we

2 You want to have burger and chips for lunch, not Irish stew.

....

....

3 You have some friends visiting you. It's time for them to go home now.

....

....

4 It's time for you and your brother to go to bed. You're playing a computer game.

....

....

5 You want to do your homework later, but your parents want you to do it now.

....

....

6 It's a cold rainy day, and your mother tells you it's time to go to school.

....

....

B Must and have to

Imagine you're in these places. What do you think you

– have to do?
– don't have to do?
– mustn't do?

You must go You have to go	=	Go!
You mustn't go	=	Don't go!
You don't have to go	=	Don't go if you don't want to.

at the theatre

You mustn't .... smoke when you're in your seat.

You don't have to .... buy a programme.

.... pay to go in.

.... wear very smart clothes.

on a train

.... have a ticket with you.

.... stay in your seat.

.... put your feet on the seats.

.... throw things out of the window.

at the beach

.... pay to go into the water.

.... put your rubbish in the bin.

.... sit in the sun.

.... park on the beach.

C Giving advice

Finish these sentences with some good advice. For each one, use two ideas from the list, and add one of your own. Use *should* and *shouldn't*.

1 If you go to the beach, *you should wear lots of sun cream, you shouldn't spend all day in the sun and you should wear a sun-hat.*

2 If you want to have good teeth, ...

3 If you're driving on a busy road, ...

4 If you want to pass a job interview, ...

5 If you want a healthy heart, ...

☐ arrive late

☐ do lots of exercise

☐ dress smartly

☐ eat fatty food

☐ eat too many sweets

☑ spend all day in the sun

☐ use a mobile phone

☐ visit the dentist regularly

☐ wear a seat belt

☑ wear lots of sun cream

Listening: *Radio phone-in*

You will hear part of a radio phone-in programme in which two experts give advice to listeners.

1 🔲 Listen to Susan's problem. Rewrite these sentences so that they are true.

Susan is a student, and she has a problem with her boyfriend, who has just got a new job. In the evening he wants to go out. She wants to stay at home and study. But he won't stay with her.

....

....

....

....

....

2 Which of these solutions do the two experts suggest?
Write *1*, *2* or – (= neither of them).

a ☐ Try to talk to him.   *e* ☐ Get divorced.

b ☐ Do what he wants.   *f* ☐ Go out with friends.

c ☐ Do what you want.   *g* ☐ Go out with another man.

d ☐ Find a way to make you both happy.

Words

Write these words in your language.

visitor   ....

pet   ....

sheets   ....

electricity ....

be quiet   ....

make a noise ....

punish   ....

steal   ....

argue   ....

Other words

....

....

....

....

A Jobs

Unscramble the letters to find the people's jobs. Then write a sentence saying what they do.
For the sentence, use one item from Box A and one from Box B.

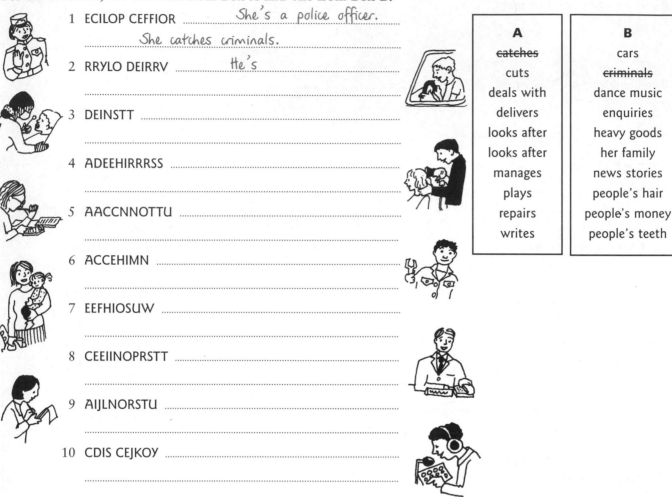

1 ECILOP CEFFIOR ..... *She's a police officer.*
   ..... *She catches criminals.*

2 RRYLO DEIRRV ..... *He's*
   .....

3 DEINSTT .....
   .....

4 ADEEHIRRRSS .....
   .....

5 AACCNNOTTU .....
   .....

6 ACCEHIMN .....
   .....

7 EEFHIOSUW .....
   .....

8 CEEIINOPRSTT .....
   .....

9 AIJLNORSTU .....
   .....

10 CDIS CEJKOY .....
   .....

A	B
~~catches~~	cars
cuts	~~criminals~~
deals with	dance music
delivers	enquiries
looks after	heavy goods
looks after	her family
manages	news stories
plays	people's hair
repairs	people's money
writes	people's teeth

B Good and bad jobs

Write about a job you'd like to have, and a job you wouldn't like to have.
Say what you would like/dislike about the job.

I'd like to be .....
.....
.....

I wouldn't like to be .....
.....
.....
.....

> I'd like to be a pilot. It's quite a difficult job, but it's very interesting, and you get a good salary. You can also travel round the world. I think pilots get long holidays, too.
> I wouldn't like to be a nurse. It's a very useful job, but it's very hard work. You have to work long hours, and you don't get much money.

C One job after another

Here's a story about someone's career. Can you unscramble the words in *italics*?

1 he wanted to be a lorry driver
2 ....
3 ....
4 ....
5 ....
6 ....
7 ....
8 ....
9 ....
10 ....
11 ....
12 ....

When Joe was a child, (1) *be driver he a wanted lorry to*, but his parents wanted him to be a businessman. When he left school, (2) *studied at he university economics*, and then (3) *a he store job department in got a*. He was good at his job, and soon (4) *him manager they advertising to promoted*. But he was bored, so (5) *job left his he* and went to live in Spain, where (6) *a in he English taught school language*. He wasn't a good teacher, and (7) *the got he sack*, and went back home. (8) *For he lot applied a jobs of*, but didn't find anything. Then one day, (9) *job an saw for a he advertisement* in his old department store: LORRY DRIVER WANTED. (10) *Went interview he an for* and (11) *got he job the*. And so in the end, (12) *driver became lorry a Joe*.

Listening: A *security guard*

You will hear an interview with a security guard. Before you listen, find out the meaning of these phrases:

a security guard   to guard a building
to break into a building   to work overtime

1 🔲 Listen to the first part and complete these sentences.

Security guards work for ....

Their job is to guard ....

They stop people ....

2 🔲 Listen to the second part and answer these questions.

a Does he always work in the same place? ....

b Does he meet people in his job? ....

c Is it interesting? ....

d Is the pay good? ....

e Can he work overtime? ....

f Does he get much free time? ....

g Does he like his job? ....

Words

Write these words in your language.

entrance ....

enquiry ....

reservation ....

pipe ....

tap (n.) ....

useful ....

salary ....

department
store ....

economics ....

career ....

Other words

....

....

....

....

....

Study pages

Check your progress

1 Choose the correct words.

a He lives ☐ somewhere ☐ anywhere in Paris, but I'm not sure where.

b I didn't go ☐ somewhere ☐ anywhere and I didn't see ☐ someone. ☐ anyone.

c I think I've got ☐ something ☐ anything in my shoe.

d There's ☐ someone ☐ anyone at the door.

2 Fill the gaps with phrases from the box. Put the verb in the correct form.

apply	
deal	after
look	for
pay	with
work	

a She's a nurse. She .... people who are ill.

b He's a receptionist in a hotel. He .... enquiries.

c I'm an accountant. I .... British Airways.

d She .... the job, but she didn't get it.

e The food's free. You don't have to .... it.

3 What do these signs mean? Complete the sentences.

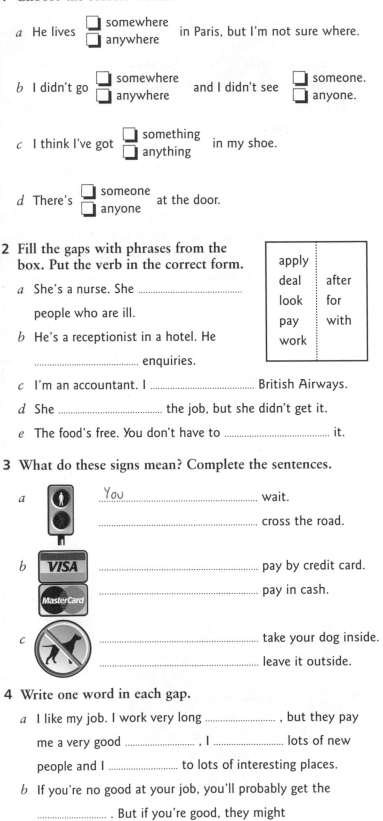

a You .... wait.

.... cross the road.

b .... pay by credit card.

.... pay in cash.

c .... take your dog inside.

.... leave it outside.

4 Write one word in each gap.

a I like my job. I work very long .... , but they pay me a very good .... , I .... lots of new people and I .... to lots of interesting places.

b If you're no good at your job, you'll probably get the .... But if you're good, they might .... you.

Phrasebook

Write this conversation in your language.

How much does it cost to rent a bike?

It's £5 an hour. Or £30 for the whole day.

....

....

Do I have to pay in advance?

No. You just give me a £10 deposit.

....

....

OK. I'll have one for the whole day, please.

....

....

Writing *Letter writing*

1 How we end a letter depends on how we begin it. Look at the examples in the box.

Beginning	Ending
Dear Sir Dear Madam Dear Sir/Madam	Yours faithfully
Dear Ms Jones Dear Mr King Dear Mrs Marple	Yours sincerely
Dear Tom Dear Fiona	Best wishes Yours Love

2 Match the beginnings and endings of the letters below. Who's writing to

a Boyd's Bookshop? ....

b Susan? ....

c Cosmos Travel? ....

d Tom? ....

Yours faithfully,
Elizabeth Burke

The Manager
Boyd's Bookshop
15 College Road
Bristol BR4 6LU

Dear Sir/Madam,

I am writing to ask you if you
which I saw in your shop last

Yours sincerely,
Douglas Trafford

Yours,
Miranda

Lots of love,
Don
x x x

Dear Susan,

I just had to write to
can't stop thinking abo
such a wonderful time
I want so much to stay

Dear Tom,

So sorry I haven't written to you for so
I've been very busy the last few weeks

Ms P Williams,
Cosmos Travel,
5 New Street,
Cardiff CF3 2BD

Dear Ms Williams

Thank you for sending
arrived yesterday. I

3 You saw this advertisement in the newspaper. Write a letter asking for more details, and saying who you are and why you are interested. Use the letter format given.

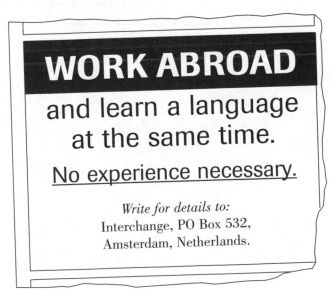

WORK ABROAD
and learn a language
at the same time.
No experience necessary.

Write for details to:
Interchange, PO Box 532,
Amsterdam, Netherlands.

```
                          Your address
                          Date
Address you're
writing to

Dear …

              Your
              letter



Ending
```

19 Telling stories

A What were they doing?

Exactly one year ago, the President died in a plane crash. Everyone remembers where they were when they heard the news, and what they were doing.

Where were these people? What do you think they were doing?

1   I was at the cinema. I was watching the new Steven Spielberg film.

PRESIDENT DIES IN PLANE CRASH

2   We were

5

3

6

4

7

B What happened next?

Write sentences with *when* or *while*. What happened next?

1   Joanna / watch TV / her flat / doorbell / ring
    Joanna was watching TV in her flat yesterday evening when the doorbell rang.
    So she opened the door. It was her mother. She had a suitcase in her hand.

2   Peter / clean / teeth / bathroom / lights / go out

3   Sam / open / front door / key / break

4   Tony and Linda / walk / river / see / man's coat / water

C Can you remember?

In the Classroom Book, you saw a man in five places. How much can you remember?
Write about what you saw. (The words in the box will help.)

At the library: He was sitting at a table, wearing sunglasses and reading
a magazine.

At the lake: ....

....

At the swimming pool: ....

....

At the theatre: ....

....

At the station: ....

....

coat
drink
fishing
flowers
hat
jacket
magazine
suitcase
sunglasses
swimsuit
tickets
towel
train
woman

Listening: *The wedding video*

You will hear a story about a wedding. Before you listen,
check that you know what these words mean:

wedding reception   cloakroom   missing
photographer   entrance hall embarrassed

Now listen and answer the questions.

1 How many people came to the reception? ....

2 What was the friend's job? ....

3 What did he do at the reception? ....

4 What did people leave in the cloakroom? ....

5 What did they find afterwards? ....

6 Who was the thief? ....

7 How did they know? ....

8 What did they do? ....

Words

Write these words in your language.

accident   ....

ladder   ....

bang   ....

push   ....

bite   ....

hurt   ....

slip   ....

trip   ....

(16th) century ....

antique shop ....

Other words

....

....

....

....

....

....

20 People

A Who's who?

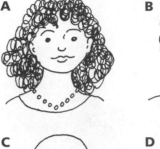

Look at the pictures. Which person:

1	[D] has a long thin face?		8	☐ has long straight hair?
2	☐ has a square face?		9	☐ has dark curly hair?
3	☐ has a round face?		10	☐ has wavy fair hair?
4	☐ has thick eyebrows?		11	☐ has a beard?
5	☐ has a pointed nose?		12	☐ has a moustache?
6	☐ has a hooked nose?		13	☐ is wearing earrings?
7	☐ is bald?		14	☐ is wearing a necklace?

B People on a train

Use the words in the boxes to describe the people in the story.

I got on the train and found my seat. There was only one other person in the compartment. He _was a short man in his 30s with curly black hair and a moustache. He was wearing a brown raincoat._ Just before the train left the station, a woman came into our compartment and sat down opposite me. She ....
....
....

At the next station, an old man got in and sat in the corner of the compartment. He ....
....
....

The next station was mine. I got off the train and telephoned Mrs Chadwick. 'I'll come and meet you in five minutes,' she said. 'How will I recognise you?' 'Well,' I said, 'I'm ....
....
.... ,'

black	moustache
short 30s	brown
curly hair	raincoat

green tall	short
fair	sunglasses
hair dress	20s

beard blue	grey
walking stick	70s
short bald	eyes

Describe yourself.

C Character adjectives

Match the sentences with the adjectives.

1 She always smiles and says hello when we meet.

2 He doesn't like giving away money.

3 She gets angry quite easily.

4 He's afraid to meet new people.

5 She often stays late at the office.

6 He always tells the truth.

7 She doesn't get upset if things go wrong.

8 He doesn't do much work.

9 She enjoys giving people presents.

10 He never remembers where he's put things.

11 She's only interested in herself.

☐ bad-tempered	☐ generous	☐ mean
☐ easy-going	☐ hard-working	☐ selfish
☐ forgetful	☐ honest	☐ shy
1 friendly	☐ lazy	

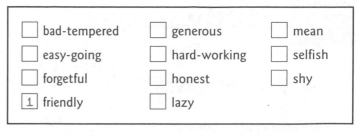

Listening: *Family picture*

1 Someone is showing you this picture of their family. Which people does he describe? Find them in the picture.

....

....

2 Write one thing about each person that you *can't* see in the picture.

a His uncle ....

b His aunt ....

c His grandfather ....

d His cousin ....

e His aunt Sophie ....

Words

Write these words in your language.

famous   ....

leader   ....

recognise   ....

razor   ....

shave   ....

smile   ....

hide   ....

alone   ....

lonely   ....

pleased   ....

Other words

....

....

....

....

....

....

....

Study pages

Check your progress

1 What are the nationalities?

a She's from Mexico. She's ....

b I'm from Greece. I'm ....

c They're from Japan. They're ....

d He's from Brazil. He's ....

e They're from Poland. They're ....

2 Complete the sentences using (1) *during* and (2) *while*.

a The phone rang three times ...

... during ....

... while ....

....

b Someone took my jewels ...

... during ....

... while ....

....

3 Here are some notes for part of a story. Write a paragraph of four sentences based on the notes.

> Sam / watch TV / bedroom / hear / noise / garden
> He / go / window / look / outside
> He / see / two men / climb / over / garden wall
> One / hold / gun

Last night, Sam ....

....

....

....

....

....

4 Continue these descriptions.

a The police are looking for ....

....

....

b The police are looking for ....

....

....

Phrasebook

Write these conversations in your language.

What do you do?

I'm a secretary.

....

....

What nationality are you?

I'm Australian.

....

....

What languages do you speak?

Arabic and French.

....

....

....

Writing *Relative clauses (1)*

1 Here are two parts of a letter written by a foreign student in Paris.

> I'm staying with my uncle. He lives just outside Paris. He's got a large house, with a beautiful garden.

> My uncle is quite rich. He works for Inter Export. It's a large company based in Paris.

We can join the sentences in each paragraph like this:

> I'm staying with my uncle, **who** lives just outside Paris. He's got a large house, with a beautiful garden.

> My uncle is quite rich. He works for Inter Export, **which** is a large company based in Paris.

We use *who* to talk about people.   We use *which* to talk about things.

Before *who* or *which* we write a comma (,) .

2 These sentences all have mistakes. Rewrite them correctly.

a I live in Stenton, it's a small village near Cambridge.

....

....

b I've got three sisters which are all older than me.

....

....

c Pandas, which they only eat bamboo, are becoming very rare.

....

....

3 Here are some more sentences from the student's letter. Fill the gaps with information from the box. Use *who* or *which*.

a I'm sending you a picture of the Pompidou Centre, ...

.... What do you think of it?

b Last night I met some old schoolfriends, ...

.... We went out for a meal together.

c I had a very interesting dish called *andouillette*, ...

....

d George sends you his best wishes. He's staying in Lyon, ...

....

e I'm spending a lot of time with a girl called Mona, ...

.... I met her at a party last weekend.

f I'm doing everything I can to improve my French, ...

....

> She's studying art here.
>
> It's a kind of sausage.
>
> It still isn't very good.
>
> They're also staying in Paris.
>
> It was built in the 70s.
>
> It's about 200 km south of here.

21 Future plans

A New Year resolutions

Read the text, and write Ebenezer's New Year resolutions. Use *going to* and *not going to*.

It was New Year's Eve. Ebenezer sat alone at home. 'Where is everyone?' he wondered. 'Why am I alone?'

'Do you really want to know?' said a voice behind his chair.

'Wh- Who's that?' cried Ebenezer.

'I am the Ghost of the New Year,' said the voice, 'and I'm going to tell you why you're alone. The problem is, you're not a very nice person. You shout at everyone. You don't smile. You never take your family out. You don't visit your friends. You spend all your money on yourself – when did you last give your children a present? And you have some very bad habits. You drink too much alcohol. You watch too much TV. You use your mobile phone in restaurants. You only have a shower once a week. And another thing. You don't …'

'All right! All right!' said Ebenezer. 'That's enough. I understand.' And he took a pen and started to write some New Year resolutions …

I'm going to be a nice person.
I'm not going to shout at people.
I'm going

B The ghost comes back

Describe Ebenezer's arrangements. Use the Present continuous and the time expressions in the box.

> this (morning)
> tomorrow (morning)
> on (Monday)
> in (three weeks)
> next (Tuesday, week)

It was Monday 1st May when the ghost came again. 'How are you?' he asked.

'Terrible!' said Ebenezer sadly. 'I haven't got any time for myself! Look. This afternoon …' And he showed the ghost these entries in his diary:

May 1st	3.00	Take children swimming
	8.00	Browns come for dinner
May 2nd	9.00	To the hairdresser's
	7.30	School concert
May 3rd		Lunch with parents-in-law
May 5th		Daughter's birthday party
May 8–12		Brother & family to stay
July 1–15		Family holiday at seaside

This afternoon he's taking the children swimming.

Listening: *Plans for the evening*

You will hear an interview with five people getting off a train. They all say what they're going to do in the evening.

1 Which people are going to do these things?
Write ✓ or ✗ in the table.

	1	2	3	4	5
A spend the evening at home					
B spend the evening at work					
C spend the evening alone					
D spend the evening with other people					

2 Which person is

a ☐ a nurse?

b ☐ a businesswoman?

c ☐ a security guard?

d ☐ a college student?

Words

Write these words in your language.

retire ....

uniform ....

type (a letter) ....

driving test ....

maybe ....

perhaps ....

Masters degree ....

(I'm) sure ....

notice board ....

arrange ....

(I'm) free ....

Other words

....

....

....

22 Around the world

A Where are they?

Here are some places from the Classroom Book unit. Use the notes to write sentences about each place.

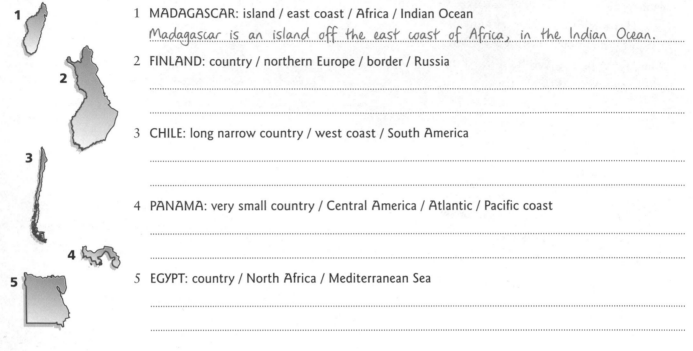

1 MADAGASCAR: island / east coast / Africa / Indian Ocean
   Madagascar is an island off the east coast of Africa, in the Indian Ocean.

2 FINLAND: country / northern Europe / border / Russia

   ....

   ....

3 CHILE: long narrow country / west coast / South America

   ....

   ....

4 PANAMA: very small country / Central America / Atlantic / Pacific coast

   ....

   ....

5 EGYPT: country / North Africa / Mediterranean Sea

   ....

   ....

Now write a sentence about one of these places (or about your own country).

6 AUSTRALIA   BRITAIN   CANADA   SOUTH AFRICA   THE UNITED STATES

....

....

B On the map

Write the missing words in the puzzle.

1 The Pacific and the Atlantic are the biggest ....s in the world.

2 The Niagara Falls are on the .... between Canada and the USA.

3 Madagascar, Java, Cuba and Tahiti are all ....s.

4 San Francisco is on the west .... of America.

5 The Nile, the Danube and the Mississippi are all ....s.

6 Everest, Mont Blanc and Kilimanjaro are all ....s.

7 .... Victoria is in East Africa; .... Superior is in Canada.

8 Vesuvius is a ....; so is Popocatepetl, and Krakatoa.

9 An area full of trees, such as the Black .... in Germany.

10 The Sahara is a ....; so is the Kalahari.

Now complete this sentence:

Europe, Asia and South America are all ....

C A good place to visit

Write about a good place to visit in your country. Include answers to these questions.

What kind of place is it?

Where is it?

How can you get there?

What can you do there?

Where can you stay?

Is it expensive?

What's the weather like?

What's the best time of the year to go there?

....

....

....

....

....

....

....

Listening: *Living in a hot climate*

You will hear a woman talking about living in Kuwait. Look at these questions. Then listen and note the woman's answers. Which questions *doesn't* she answer?

1 Is it always hot in Kuwait?

....

2 Which are the hottest months?

....

3 When is the coolest time of year?

....

4 Is it humid?

....

5 Does it ever rain?

....

6 Do most buildings have air-conditioning (a/c)?

....

7 Is it too hot to drive a car?

....

8 Do you ever need warm clothes?

....

9 Is the sea pleasant to swim in?

....

Words

Write these words in your language.

fairly ....

partly ....

narrow ....

thousands of (people) ....

flat ....

mountainous ....

hardly ever ....

diving ....

whale ....

shark ....

Other words

....

....

....

....

....

Check your progress

1 Rewrite these sentences. Change the phrases in *italics*.

a There wasn't *anyone* in the building.
   There was

b They ate *nothing* for three days.

c 'Sit down,' he said. '*You're going nowhere.*'

d I can't come because I *haven't got any* money.

2 Do you think these speakers are talking about

   1 now?   2 around now?   3 the future?

Mark the sentences *1, 2* or *3*.

a ☐ We're coming on Monday.

b ☐ Shh! I'm talking on the phone.

c ☐ We're playing tennis a lot these days.

d ☐ You're not doing enough exercise.

e ☐ We're giving her a jumper for her birthday.

3 Read the text. What are Jill and Tim going to do (and not going to do) while they're on holiday?

> Jill and Tim hate getting up early to go to work. Jill hates typing letters, and Tim hates wearing a suit. They both love lying in the sun. Tim likes reading magazines, and Jill enjoys swimming. Next week, they're going away for their summer holiday.

a They

b Jill

c Tim

d They

e Tim

f Jill

4 Fill the gaps.

a France is in .... Japan is in ....

   Argentina is in .... Kenya is in ....

b The Pacific .... , the Mediterrranean ....

c The .... of the world is more than six billion.

Phrasebook

Write this conversation in your language.

Writing *Relative clauses (2)*

1 Here is some information about India. We can join the ideas together using relative clauses.

Bombay is one of India's main sea ports. (***It***'s on the west coast.) →	Bombay, ***which*** is on the west coast, is one of India's main sea ports.
Jawaharlal Nehru died in 1964. (***He*** was the first prime minister of India.) →	Jawaharlal Nehru, ***who*** was the first prime minister of India, died in 1964.
200 km from the capital Delhi is the town of Agra. (The Taj Mahal was built ***there*** in 1653.) →	200 km from the capital Delhi is the town of Agra, ***where*** the Taj Mahal was built in 1653.

2 Join the ideas in brackets ( ) to the main sentence using a relative clause.

  a Jakarta has a population of about ten million. (It's the capital of Indonesia.)

  ....

  ....

  ....

  b The Cape Verde Islands have been independent since 1975. (They were once a Portuguese colony.)

  ....

  ....

  c In the square there is a statue of Charles I. (He was King of England from 1625 to 1649.)

  ....

  ....

3 Join these ideas together so that they make a paragraph of four or five sentences. Use *who, which, where* and *and*.

If you have time, you should visit the Parrot Café. It's in a small side street behind the harbour. It's the oldest café in the town. It's very popular with fishermen. They sit there all day playing cards. The owner is in his 80s. He's a retired sea captain. Next to the Parrot Café there's a small museum. You can see treasure from an old sailing ship there. It sank near the town in the 17th century.

....

....

....

....

....

....

....

....

....

....

23 Past and present

A Everything has changed

These people's lives have changed. Write about the changes, using the Present perfect tense.

1

Three months ago, Rita was still at school, studying for her exams. She didn't wear glasses, and she was saving up for a new computer. Now, everything's changed …

a (leave) *She's left school.*

b (take) *She's taken her exams.*

c (start) ....

d (buy) ....

2

Two years ago, Colin and Mary were still engaged, and they didn't live in London. They didn't have any children, and Julia was working. Now, everything's changed …

a (get) ....

b (move) ....

c (have) ....

d (stop) ....

3

Three months ago, Oliver was in prison. He had a beard, but not a moustache, and he was writing a book about his life. Now everything's changed …

a (come out) ....

b (grow) ....

c (shave off) ....

d (finish) ....

B The answer's 'No'

Here are some answers. What are the questions?
Use the Present perfect tense.

1 Q *Have you had your lunch yet?*
....

A No, we're still eating.

2 Q *Has she* ....

A No, she's still here.

3 Q ....

A No, they're still in bed.

4 Q ....

A No, I'm still looking for it.

5 Q ....

A No, he's still out.

6 Q ....

A No, I'm still reading it.

No, we're still waiting for it.

7 Q ....

A No, we're still waiting for it.

8 Q ....

A No, he's still single.

9 Q ....

A No, they're still living in the same place.

C ... but ...

What have you done so far in your life? What haven't you done? Write about the topics on the right.

> The verb go has two past participles:
> He's gone to Paris. (= he's there now)
> He's been to Paris. (= he went and came back)

> I've never eaten sushi, but I've eaten octopus.

> I've eaten shish kebabs, but I've never eaten sushi.

> I've eaten sushi but I've never eaten moussaka.

1 I've ....

....

.... eat sushi

2 ....

.... fly in Concorde

3 ....

.... drink vodka

4 ....

.... play rugby

5 ....

.... go to Hawaii

....

Listening: *Have you ever ...?*

1 Four people talk about the things in the pictures. What are the four questions?

 motorbike    sailing boat   ostrich   Shakespeare

2 Listen again and answer the questions.

1 *a* How old was she? ....

  b What did her brother do? ....

     What didn't he do? ....

  c How did she feel? ....

2 *a* How old was he? ....

  b Who did he go with? ....

  c What was the weather like? ....

3 *a* What does the burger bar sell? ....

  b What do they taste like? ....

  c How often does he eat them? ....

4 *a* What did she see? ....

  b When did she see it? ....

  c What did she think of it? ....

Words

Write these words in your language.

pretty (boring) ....

temporary ....

grow (a beard) ....

start (smoking) ....

stop (smoking) ....

caravan ....

helicopter ....

rabbit ....

passport ....

move into (a flat) ....

move out of (a flat) ....

Other words

....

....

....

24 Arts and entertainment

A Who, what and where?

The answers in this crossword come from the whole unit. Letters in brackets ( ) are scrambled answers.

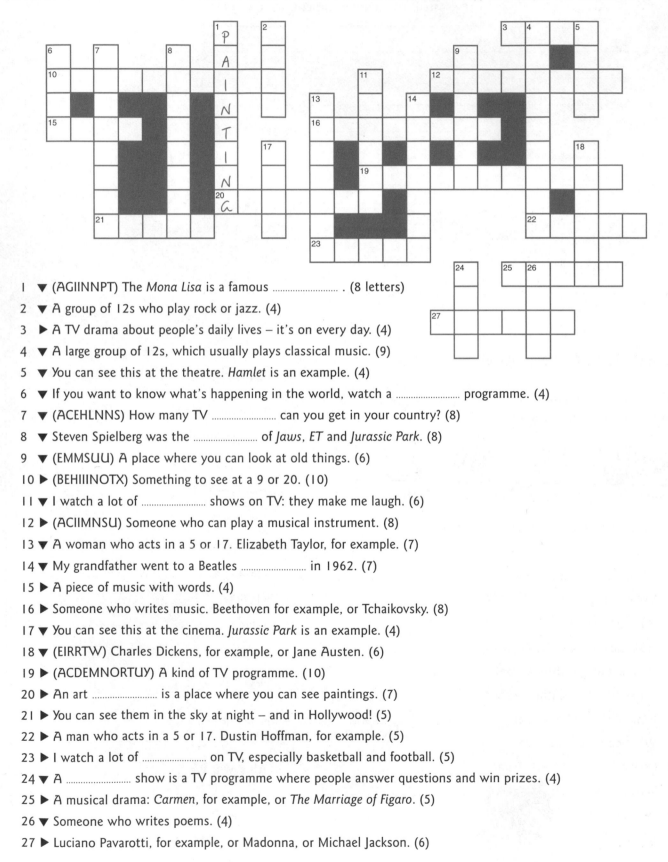

1 ▼ (AGIINNPT) The *Mona Lisa* is a famous .... (8 letters)

2 ▼ A group of 12s who play rock or jazz. (4)

3 ▶ A TV drama about people's daily lives – it's on every day. (4)

4 ▼ A large group of 12s, which usually plays classical music. (9)

5 ▼ You can see this at the theatre. *Hamlet* is an example. (4)

6 ▼ If you want to know what's happening in the world, watch a .... programme. (4)

7 ▼ (ACEHLNNS) How many TV .... can you get in your country? (8)

8 ▼ Steven Spielberg was the .... of *Jaws*, *ET* and *Jurassic Park*. (8)

9 ▼ (EMMSUU) A place where you can look at old things. (6)

10 ▶ (BEHIIINOTX) Something to see at a 9 or 20. (10)

11 ▼ I watch a lot of .... shows on TV: they make me laugh. (6)

12 ▶ (ACIIMNSU) Someone who can play a musical instrument. (8)

13 ▼ A woman who acts in a 5 or 17. Elizabeth Taylor, for example. (7)

14 ▼ My grandfather went to a Beatles .... in 1962. (7)

15 ▶ A piece of music with words. (4)

16 ▶ Someone who writes music. Beethoven for example, or Tchaikovsky. (8)

17 ▼ You can see this at the cinema. *Jurassic Park* is an example. (4)

18 ▼ (EIRRTW) Charles Dickens, for example, or Jane Austen. (6)

19 ▶ (ACDEMNORTUY) A kind of TV programme. (10)

20 ▶ An art .... is a place where you can see paintings. (7)

21 ▶ You can see them in the sky at night – and in Hollywood! (5)

22 ▶ A man who acts in a 5 or 17. Dustin Hoffman, for example. (5)

23 ▶ I watch a lot of .... on TV, especially basketball and football. (5)

24 ▼ A .... show is a TV programme where people answer questions and win prizes. (4)

25 ▶ A musical drama: *Carmen*, for example, or *The Marriage of Figaro*. (5)

26 ▼ Someone who writes poems. (4)

27 ▶ Luciano Pavarotti, for example, or Madonna, or Michael Jackson. (6)

B Likes and dislikes

What do you like in the world of arts and entertainment? What don't you like? Write about *five* things.

> I love the Harry Potter books. They're for children, but adults read them too. I think they're very exciting stories.

> I don't mind opera. The music's good, but I can never understand the words. And some operas are too long!

> I hate soaps. They're boring, and the actors aren't usually very good.

1 I love ....

....

2 I like ....

....

3 I don't mind ....

....

4 I don't like ....

....

5 I hate ....

....

art
books
films
museums
music
theatre
TV

Listening: *TV survey*

1 Five people say what they like and don't like about TV programmes in Britain. Who says these things? Write *1, 2, 3, 4, 5* or – (= no one).

a ☐ Most news programmes are too serious.

b ☐ Good films should be on earlier in the evening.

c ☐ There isn't much good new music on TV.

d ☐ There should be more classical music, and less pop music.

e ☐ There isn't enough sport on Saturdays.

f ☐ There should be more international news.

2 Which speaker mentions these things? What does he/she say about them?

a ☐ a war in Africa ....

b ☐ ordinary pop music ....

c ☐ Saturday afternoon ....

d ☐ foreign films ....

e ☐ teenagers ....

Words

Write these words in your language.

symphony ....

well known ....

(quiz) show ....

What's on? ....

billion ....

romantic ....

musical (n.) ....

live (football) ....

star (n.) ....

star (v.) ....

Other words

....

....

....

....

Final review

Sentences (12 points)

Complete the sentences so they mean the same.

Example: His flat's got two bathrooms.

There are two bathrooms in his flat.

1 Is there a restaurant in this hotel?

Has ....

2 I've had this car for ten years.

.... ten years ago.

3 They moved to London in 1990.

.... since 1990.

4 Their TV was cheaper than ours.

Our TV ....

5 We went nowhere.

.... anywhere.

6 You can stay in bed.

.... get up.

Lists (10 points)

Add to these lists.

Examples: living room, kitchen, _bedroom bathroom_

wife, _husband_ ; son, _daughter_

1 aunt, ... ; nephew, ...

2 chicken, beef, ...

3 aubergine, cabbage, potato, ...

....

4 _He's wearing_ a hat, ...

....

5 _She's wearing_ a jacket, ...

....

6 shy, bad-tempered, forgetful, ...

....

Verbs (18 points)

Fill the gaps, using the verbs in brackets.

Example: I (go) .....went..... to the party last night,

but I (not see) _didn't see_ your friends.

1 I'm completely different from my sister Sue. She (enjoy)

.... cooking, but she (not play) ....

any sports. I (love) .... sports, but I (not like)

.... cooking at all.

2 Ed is a writer. He (write) .... children's books.

At the moment, he (write) .... a book about

King Arthur and the Round Table.

3 If I (see) .... them at school tomorrow, I

(invite) .... them to the party.

4 He's nearly ready to go out. He (have) .... a

shower and he (get) .... dressed , but he (not

drink) .... his coffee yet.

5 Last night, I (drive) .... home from work when

a dog (run) .... in front of my car. Fortunately,

I (not hit) .... it.

6 I (never eat) .... rabbit in my life, but I

(eat) .... ostrich. I (have) .... an

ostrich burger at a party last weekend.

7 Sorry. I can't play tennis tomorrow because

I (go) .... for an interview.

Words in context (20 points)

Write _one_ word in each gap.

1 Some time soon you'll ....

a tall, dark stranger, you'll ....

in love, and you'll .... married.

2 I usually catch the early morning train. It ....

Newcastle at 6.25 and .... in London at about

8.30. So the whole .... takes about two hours.

3 They live on the 10th floor of a big .... of flats.

Their living room .... south, so they have a

wonderful .... of the mountains.

4 – Excuse me. What .... is that coat?

   – It's 42. Would you like to .... it on?

   – Yes, please ... How does it look?

   – It looks very good. It really .... you.

5 In football you .... the ball,
   in basketball you .... it,
   and in tennis, you .... it with
   a racket.

6 If you're no good at your job, you'll get the ....
   But if you're good, they'll .... you – and then
   you'll get more money!

7 Portugal is in south-western
   .... It has a ....
   with Spain, and it's on the
   Atlantic ....

Questions (20 points)

Here are some answers. What are the questions?

Example: Q *Where do you live?* ....

         A (I live) In Vienna.

1 Q ....
   A (I've got) Three (televisions).

2 Q ....
   A (It takes) About two hours.

3 Q ....
   A (She left) Yesterday morning.

4 Q ....
   A No, he hasn't (finished work yet).

5 Q ....
   A (They'll get to the station) By taxi.

6 Q ....
   A Yes, there will (be a test on Friday).

7 Q ....
   A No, we don't (have to pay to go in).

8 Q ....
   A (They're going to stay) At a friend's flat.

9 Q ....
   A (I'm having) Moussaka (for lunch).

10 Q ....
   A No (I've never been to Toronto).

Prepositions (10 points)

Write prepositions in the gaps.

Example: Who's going to pay ......*for*...... the meal?

1 I usually go to work .... bus.

2 I saw him .... Tuesday. He came to my flat
   .... six o'clock .... the morning.

3 You can pay .... cheque.

4 Carry on .... this street, go .... the
   supermarket, and then turn right. You'll see the
   museum .... your left.

5 Police are looking .... a man .... his
   late 50s .... long grey hair and a beard.

6 You should eat plenty .... fruit. It's very good
   .... you.

7 I work .... a computer company. I'm a
   receptionist. I deal .... phone enquiries and I
   look .... visitors.

8 San Francisco is .... California. It's ....
   the west coast.

9 I'm not very good .... mending things.

10 He woke up three times .... the night.

Tables (10 points)

1 Write opposites.

   big   *small*   cheap   *expensive*
   quiet   .... tidy   ....
   clean   .... dark   ....

2 Write nationalities

   India   *Indian*   England *English*
   Italy   .... Germany ....
   China   .... Spain   ....

3 Write past simple and past participle forms.

   write   *wrote*   *written*
   leave   ....
   take   ....
   come   ....

4 Write comparative and superlative forms.

   cheap   *cheaper*   *cheapest*
   friendly ....
   popular   ....
   good   ....

Tapescripts

Unit 1 The best time of the day

1 For me, the best time of the day is the morning. I really like getting up early, usually around 6, 6.30, and I put on my running clothes and go for a run. Then I come back and have a shower, and then my husband gets up and we have breakfast together.

2 One time of the day I really enjoy is my lunch break. I nearly always use it to go to the shops. Sometimes I buy things, but often I just look around. And if it's nice weather, I walk round the streets. I love being away from the office, just having an hour to myself.

3 The time I like best is late at night, after midnight. I never want to go to bed, I really enjoy being awake at that time of night. Usually I study at night, but I also like talking – friends come round and we just sit and talk. I suppose that's one good thing about being a student – you don't have to get up in the morning.

Unit 2 Relatives

1 The oldest person in my family is my grandmother. She's 90 years old, but she's still very active. She has her own flat in London, she can still walk, she reads a lot, she watches TV – we all really like her.

2 The most interesting person in my family is probably my brother, because he has a really interesting job – he's an airline pilot, and he travels all over the world. He's very nice – he always brings back presents from the countries he goes to.

3 The richest person in my family is definitely my uncle. He sells cars, and he's got lots of money – very rich. He's got a big house in the country, with a swimming pool, and a big car, obviously. He doesn't really enjoy life, I don't think – he works all the time, never has a holiday, and he's very mean, never gives us presents ... I don't really like him very much.

Unit 3 Rooms and flats

1 A Hello. I'm phoning about the room you have to rent.
  B Yes.
  A Is it still free?
  B Yes, it is, yes.
  A Could you tell me something about it?

B Yes, it's on the top floor, it's quite a small room, but it's fine for one person – it's just for you, is it?
A That's right, yes.
B OK, well, it's got a desk by the window, a bed, a cupboard, and there's a chair ...
A What about the bathroom?
B Yes, well there's a bathroom on the same floor.
A Oh, OK. Could I come and look at it?
B Yes, certainly, when would you ...

2 A Hello. I saw your advertisement for a flat in the paper.
  B Yes ...
  A How many rooms has it got?
  B Three rooms altogether, a living room and two bedrooms, and also a kitchen and a bathroom.
  A OK. Now, it's on the 3rd floor ...
  B That's right.
  A Is there a lift?
  B No, I'm afraid there isn't a lift, it's quite an old building.
  A I see. And have the rooms got balconies?
  B One room has a small balcony, but not the others.
  A I see. Now, you say it's near the city centre. Where is it exactly?
  B It's just by the railway station.
  A Oh. OK, well, I'll think about it. Thanks.

Unit 4 Trip to Stonehenge

A Can I help you?
B Yes. I want to visit Stonehenge. What's the best way to go there?
A OK. Do you have a car?
B No.
A OK, in that case the best way is to go by coach. There are tours which leave every morning – when do you want to go?
B Tomorrow, if possible.
A Right. There's a coach which leaves at 9.30, and it gets to Stonehenge at about 11.30. Then you have a few hours there and it comes back in the afternoon.
B Oh, it's quite a long way, then.
A Yes, it's about 150 kilometres.
B Hmm. How much does it cost?
A £32 return.
B What about the train? Is there a train?
A No, you can't really get there by train because Stonehenge isn't near a station, unfortunately. You could rent a car.

B How much does that cost?
A About £50 probably, for a day.
B OK, thanks. I'll think about it.

Unit 5 We're busy

1 Some friends are coming to stay with us tonight and for the weekend. They're quite a big family, and at the moment we're moving mattresses into all the rooms because we haven't got enough beds for them all. There'll be eight of us altogether, no, nine. And one of my children has got 'flu so nobody can sleep in his room. So they'll be sleeping in the sitting room and in the dining room and in my study. So we're, as I say, moving mattresses about. We are looking for a new house at the moment because we just don't find ours big enough if we're going to have people to stay all the time.

2 Well, at the moment I'm working really hard for my exams. They're in about three months' time, so I'm reading a lot at the moment but it's all for my exams. It'll be really nice to read a good novel when the exams are over. And then I'm going to start looking for a job, and I really don't know what'll happen then.

Unit 6 Polish dishes

A Well, what have we got to eat here?
B Well, this is a dish called *bigos*. All you need to make bigos is sweet cabbage and a sour cabbage, and some pieces of cooked meat – different ones, whatever you have at hand, really. And there is one thing you really have to have, which is smoked bacon. Then you just cook the cabbage, then you mix all those things together. You put a lot of spices, you can add some tomatoes, and you just stew it very slowly. And the more times you reheat it the better it is.

And this is *chlodnik*. This is a soup, which you make of young beetroots. You just chop young beetroots, including leaves, and you just cook it as an ordinary soup. Then you add some generous amount of cream, and you serve it cool with some boiled eggs, which is a perfect dish for a hot summer day.

Unit 7 A man and a penguin

One morning a man found a penguin outside his front door. He took the penguin to the police station, and the policeman told him to take the penguin to the zoo. So the man said OK, and off he went with the penguin.

That evening, the policeman saw the man with the penguin again, at a bus stop. 'Hey,' he said, 'I told you to take that penguin to the zoo.'

'Oh yes,' said the man, 'I took him to the zoo – he really enjoyed it, and now we're going to the cinema.'

Unit 8 Favourite rooms

1 My favourite room is a room I have under the house, in the cellar, which is where I listen to music. It's quite a big room, and it's got hardly any furniture – just an old sofa, an old carpet, a bookshelf full of CDs and cassettes, and (the most important thing) a stereo with two very big speakers. And it's great, I can sit down there and play music very loud, and no one else can hear it.

2 My favourite room is my daughter's bedroom. It's very small – it's actually the smallest room in the whole flat, but it's very bright and sunny and it's full of all her things. It's got a wooden bed, and a wooden cupboard, and there's a shelf which runs all round the room and has all her toys on it. And there's a chair by the window where you can sit and read. It's a lovely room, very warm and comfortable.

Unit 9 What has happened?

1 A What are you doing?
   B I've lost my glasses. I had them a minute ago. Maybe they're behind here.
   A Have you looked in your pocket?
   B Yes, I have.
   A Hmm. What about the … Oh, hey, here they are, on the table!
   B Oh, thanks.

2 A Hey, what's that ring? Is it new?
   B Yes. I've just got engaged.
   A Engaged? I didn't even know you had a boyfriend.
   B No, well I didn't, at least … well, we met this summer. On holiday – in Spain.
   A Well – congratulations!

3 A Hi! Where's your car?
   B I haven't got a car any more. I've sold it.
   A Sold it? Why?
   B I didn't really need a car. So now I go everywhere by bike – it's much better.

4 A What's happened to your arm?
   B I've broken it.
   A Oh dear – how did you do that?
   B Well, I was on my bike, and this car came out suddenly and I fell off. I had to go to hospital.

Unit 10 Working clothes

1 Well, I don't have to go to an office, I work at home, so I just wear comfortable clothes – jeans, T-shirts, jumpers, things like that. If I go to a meeting, then maybe I'll wear a jacket – certainly not a tie, though.

2 I visit customers – I sell computer equipment – so I have to wear fairly smart clothes. I usually wear a skirt or a dress, or sometimes trousers – but not jeans, I couldn't wear jeans in my job.

3 Well, I work in a bank, and I always wear a suit, like everyone else. I wear a shirt and tie, of course, and black shoes and socks. I like wearing a suit – I think they look good.

Unit 11 A healthy diet

1 I'm not actually a vegetarian, but I hardly eat any meat. I eat fish, but not very often, maybe once a week. I eat a lot of vegetables and a lot of fruit – I really like fruit, I have it for breakfast every day. Fat – yes, I do eat quite a lot of fat – olive oil, butter as well, milk, yeah. But I don't eat very many sweet things – I don't like cakes, I have chocolate sometimes, but not very often.

2 Well, I must say I eat quite a lot of sweet things – not too much, but I do like eating cakes and biscuits, and I have sugar in coffee too. I eat quite a lot of fruit, but not many vegetables – I don't really like vegetables, except potatoes. I like meat, I eat a lot of meat, every day, probably – but I don't eat fish at all, I hate fish. Fat, yes, I probably eat too much fat – I really love butter and cream, and of course meat has a lot of fat in it as well.

Unit 12 Ouch!

1 A Ooh, could you drive?
   B Why, what's the matter?
   A My neck aches, for some reason. It really hurts.
   B Oh dear. How did that happen?
   A I don't know. I just woke up this morning and it started hurting. Ooh!
   B OK, I'll drive then, no problem.
   A Thanks.

2 A Be careful here, it's wet … Careful! Oh! Are you all right?
   B Yes, I think so. Ooh! Ooh, my knee hurts.
   A Try to stand up.
   B Ooh!
   A OK?
   B No, it really hurts. I can't stand up. I think I've broken it.

3 A Ah, my head!
   B Have you got a headache?
   A Yeah, it was all that cigarette smoke at that party. Always gives me a headache.
   B Oh dear. Do you want an aspirin?
   A No, I think I'll just go and lie down for a bit.

Unit 13 Giving blood

OK, well, don't worry, there's nothing much to it, really. You go into a room and there'll be a nurse there. And first of all she'll take a sample of your blood, because they need to know what blood group you belong to, so she'll take a tiny bit of blood from the end of your finger.

Then you lie down, and the nurse will put a needle into your arm, and the blood will go through the needle and into a bag beside you. You don't have to do anything – just lie there and relax. And it won't hurt – well, maybe just a bit at the beginning when the needle goes in, but after that you won't feel anything at all. And they take about half a litre of blood – but you've got five litres, so it won't make much difference to you.

And that's it, the whole thing will take about half an hour, probably. You might feel a bit weak afterwards for a time, so you might want to lie down, have a rest for a bit, but you'll soon feel quite normal again.

Unit 14 Living in London

1 Well, I like living in London, mainly because I live right in the centre. If I want to go to the theatre, I can leave my flat about 15 minutes before the play starts and walk to the theatre. I can do the same with the cinema. In the morning I can get up, go out, sit in a café, read the paper, meet friends – there's a wonderful atmosphere, it feels like a big city and I really like that.

2 I don't like living in London at all. We've got a small house with a very small garden, and there's a railway line at the bottom of the garden, so it's very noisy. We're near the airport, so aeroplanes go over every two minutes – so you

can't sit outside because there are trains and planes. And it's very dirty as well. My journey to work is terrible, I hate it – I have to go by underground. It's full of people, you can never get a seat, and it's just the same going home in the evening. I think living out in the country must be much nicer.

Unit 15 The most and the fewest

1 A I'm afraid I only speak English, and a little school French, I only really speak English.
B I've got a Spanish father and as a boy I learnt both Spanish and English. I also can speak French quite well and Italian, and I'm not bad at German either.
C I learnt French and German at school, but wasn't very good, but good enough to be able to go to France or Germany and get by and be able to have a conversation.
2 A Oh, I've travelled a lot – I've been to most of the countries in Europe, I've also been to Canada and at the same time went to the United States of America, and also down to Mexico, which was lovely.
B I'm sorry to say I've never ever been outside Britain. I must do it some time.
C I've been very lucky, because my parents worked for one of the airlines, and I've been able to travel. I've travelled to Australia and to Japan, and last year we went to China.

Unit 16 Rock climbing

Part 1
A Why do you like rock climbing?
B Well, I like it because it's exciting. But I also like it because you have to think. You look at this wall of rock and you really have to think hard, you have to concentrate. You don't think about anything else at all, you forget about all your problems, your work, everything – you just think how to climb this rock, how to get to the top, how to stay alive. And that's great.
A Don't you ever feel frightened?
B Oh yeah, every time.

Part 2
A When did you feel most frightened?
B Well, once I was in Italy, in the Alps, and I fell. And it wasn't a very steep slope, so I didn't just fall, I bounced and I slithered all the way down the slope. And I

kept thinking, 'I'm going to hurt myself, the next time I'm going to hurt myself', all the way down. And I thought, 'Maybe the rope's going to break', and – well, I had lots of time to feel frightened.
A And did you hurt yourself?
B No, I was lucky. I hurt myself a bit, but not much.

Unit 17 Radio phone-in

A And we have Susan on the phone, who's phoning us from Woking. Susan, can you hear?
B Yes, I can. Hello.
A Hello, Susan. What's your problem?
B Well, you see the thing is, I have a very good relationship with my husband, we've been married about five years now, but a few months ago he got a new job. And he works very hard, and all he wants to do is sit in front of the TV and go to sleep.
A I see.
B Well, I work too, but what I want to do in the evenings is to go out and have some fun and relax a bit, and you know, he won't come with me, he really won't, and I just don't know what to do.
A OK. Chris, have you got any ideas how we can help Susan?
C Yes. Susan, I would suggest you actually talk to him about the problem. Talk to him – see if you can get him to come out with you shall we say for two nights in the week, and then you perhaps stay at home watching TV for the other nights. Talk about it, and try to find something you both want.
D Susan, if I can come in here. What I would suggest is – I don't know if you've tried this, but maybe you should go out with some friends on your own – you know, some girlfriends or something, to the cinema, say. If he wants to stay at home, that's fine, but I don't think you should let him stop you from doing what you want.
A There you are, Susan, I hope that's helped you, and from all of us here we very much hope that you sort things out quickly. OK, we're moving on now to Sharon, who's calling us from …

Unit 18 A security guard

Part 1
A Can you tell me what sort of work you do?
B Yeah, I'm a security guard.
A I see. What does that involve?

B Well, we work for companies, and we guard their buildings during the day, sometimes during the night. That's what we do, we stop people breaking into the building.

Part 2
A What do you enjoy about your job?
B Well, it's always a bit different, you don't always work in the same place, so you travel a bit. You meet people, people are mostly very friendly …
A Anything you don't like about it?
B Oh, quite a lot, yeah. The pay isn't very good. It's not a very interesting job, can be very boring in fact, and I have to work very long hours.
A So you don't get much free time?
B That's right. Not if you work overtime, which is really how you earn enough money.
A And how much is that?
B Well, if you want to earn, say, £400 a week, you have to work, ooh, at least 70, 80 hours a week.
A Ooh, that's a long week.
B It is, yeah.

Unit 19 The wedding video

When I got married, we had a big wedding party afterwards, a reception, in a beautiful old hotel. It was a big reception, about 100 people came, and a friend of mine was a photographer, and he made a video of the whole wedding, and during the reception he walked around taking pictures all over the hotel.

There was a cloakroom by the entrance where people left their coats, and a few people left money in their coats – it was a private party, so I suppose they thought it was all right. But afterwards, quite a few of these people found that their money was missing. Well, no one knew how it happened, so of course we couldn't do anything about it.

Well anyway, a few days later this friend of mine, the photographer, started looking through the video and choosing the best bits, to make a film of the wedding. And there were some pictures he took in the entrance hall, and in one of these pictures, a man suddenly appeared, came out of the cloakroom, walked quickly across the hall and out of the house. He never looked at the camera, and I guess my friend didn't notice him at the time – but you could see clearly in the pictures that his pockets were absolutely full of things.

In fact it was one of the guests, some cousin of my wife's. So what we did was, we went to visit him, and we played him this part of the video. He was very embarrassed of course, and he gave everything back – well, nothing else he could do, really.

Unit 20 Family picture

1 That's my uncle – he's the tall one with the round face and the moustache and the small nose. He's a dentist – everyone says he's very rich. His wife's a dentist as well – that's her standing next to him, the woman with the glasses and the short fair hair.

2 Now the old man with the stick – the bald one with the thin face – that's my grandfather. He's very old now, 88, I think he is. He lives a few streets away from us.

3 And do you see the man in his late twenties, the one with the long hair and the beard, with the big nose? That's my cousin Adam. He's a musician, he's in Japan at the moment. He's learning to play Japanese music.

4 Now you see that tall woman with the curly hair and the round glasses? The one with the long earrings? That's my aunt Sophie – she's my father's sister. She lives in Miami, she's the manager of a hotel there.

Unit 21 Plans for the evening

1 Well, I'm on night duty at a factory near here, so that's where I'm going now. I don't have to do much, I just have to be there and keep an eye on things. So I've got a small TV there. I'll probably watch a bit of TV or video, read the paper, and then I'll sleep for a bit.

2 Well, I'm going round to a friend's house first, and a few other people are coming too and then we're all going out to a café or somewhere. Then there's a big party up at the college, so we're all going up there after that.

3 I'm in the middle of painting my bedroom, so that's what I'm going to do this evening – I'm selling my flat next week, so I want to get it finished by the weekend.

4 I'm going to get a pizza, take it home and eat it, go to bed, read for a bit and then go to sleep – I've been on duty at the hospital since 6 o'clock this morning. I'm really tired, I just feel like going to bed early.

5 Well, first I'm going to my Portuguese class, it's an evening class. I'm going to Brazil on business next month, so I'm learning Portuguese. After that – I don't know. Usually some of the people from the class go for a drink together, so I'll probably do that.

Unit 22 Living in a hot climate

I think the hottest place I've ever lived in is Kuwait, in the Arabian Gulf. It's certainly very hot most of the year, but particularly in July and August, of course – it can reach up to 53 degrees centigrade in late July. It's a dry heat rather than a humid one, though, so you're not as hot as you would be, say, in England perhaps if it reached 50 degrees. And of course everything is air-conditioned, the schools are air-conditioned, every office is air-conditioned, your houses are air-conditioned, so you just basically drive to a place with your a/c on in the car, leap out, run into your school or your office, stay there all day, usually having to put a jacket on because it's often really quite cool inside, then you jump back into your car again and drive home. The water's often too hot to swim in, the sea water, that is, during the summer. It's usually too hot even to sunbathe in the middle of summer – you just feel that your skin is sizzling.

Unit 23 Have you ever ...?

1 A Have you ever ridden a motorbike?
  B Yes, I have – once. It was when I was 15, and my brother had a motorbike, and I really wanted to try it. So I got on it and he started the engine for me and off I went. But he didn't tell me how to stop it. And I went round and round this square where we lived, about four times I think it was, and in end I managed to stop. But I was very frightened, and I've never been on a motorbike since.

2 A Have you ever been sailing?
  B Yes, quite a few times, actually. The first time was on my tenth birthday. My uncle and aunt had a sailing boat, and they took me out in it for my birthday. And I remember it was beautiful sunny weather, not too much wind, and I really enjoyed it.

3 A Have you ever eaten ostrich?
  B Yes, actually I quite often eat it. There's a burger bar near us, and they sell ostrich burgers – I have one about once a week probably. They taste really good – something between chicken and beef. They're supposed to be quite good for you as well, because they don't have much fat in them.

4 A Have you ever seen a play by Shakespeare?
  B Yes, of course I have – in fact I saw one last weekend. I was up in London for the weekend, and I went with some friends to see *Hamlet*. It was really good – I enjoyed it.

Unit 24 TV survey

1 I think there should be more programmes about new bands and music. There's plenty of ordinary pop music, but you don't hear much good new music, good rock bands, good jazz – there are so many good new bands, but you never see them on TV, I don't know why.

2 Well, I think there should be more news programmes for young people. All the news is very good, but it's so serious and boring, it isn't really very interesting for teenagers, say, or younger people.

3 I think there's far too much sport, especially at the weekend. On Saturday afternoon, all you can watch is sport – it's too much. There should be something for people who don't like sport so much.

4 I think it's a pity that all the good films seem to be on so late at night, especially foreign films – they always seem to be on after 10 o'clock, or midnight sometimes. I don't know who's still awake at that time, I'm certainly not.

5 Well, the news – I think it's very good, but it's nearly all about what's happening in Britain. Like, if a famous actor gets married, that's on the news, but if there's a war in Africa somewhere, that's not on the news. I think that's wrong.

Answer key

Unit 1 Things people do

A Positive and negative

1 They watch old films, but they don't watch news programmes.
2 She goes to parties, but she doesn't go to the theatre.
3 They use a typewriter, but they don't use a computer.
4 She drinks wine, but she doesn't smoke.
5 They play chess, but they don't play basketball.
6 She likes dogs, but she doesn't like cats.

C Asking Wh- questions

2 Where do they live?
3 What do crocodiles eat?
4 Where does she park her car?
5 What time / When do you have lunch?
6 How much (money) do you want?
7 Why does he walk to work?
8 When do you use English?

Listening: The best time of the day

1 Early morning. Gets up around 6.30, goes for a run.
2 Lunch break. Goes to the shops, walks round the streets.
3 Late at night (after midnight). Studies, talks to friends.
Speaker 3 is a student.
Speaker 2 works in an office.
Speaker 1 is married.

Unit 2 Family and friends

A Family tree

1 grandfather	12 brother-in-law
2 grandmother	13 nephew
3 aunt	14 niece
4 uncle	15 daughter-in-law
5 mother	
6 father	16 son
7 mother-in-law	17 daughter
8 father-in-law	18 son-in-law
9 sister-in-law	19 grandson
10 brother	20 granddaughter
11 sister	

Not used: cousin

Listening: Relatives

1 She's 90. She has her own flat. She can still walk.
2 He's an airline pilot. He travels all over the world. He has an interesting job.
3 He sells cars. He has one house. He never goes on holiday.

Study pages A

Check your progress

1 three hundred and sixty-five.
  (the) 15th (of) January nineteen ninety-nine.
  (a) quarter to twelve or eleven forty-five.
2 *a* ... my parents' bedroom
  b ... my sister's bedroom
  c ... Harry's bedroom
  d ... the children's bedroom
3 *a* asleep   *c* get up
  b wake up   *d* get undressed
4 A Do you work in Cambridge?
  B Yes. I work in a bookshop.
  A ... Where does she work?
  B She works at the university.
  A ... What does she teach?
  B She doesn't teach.
    She works in a/the library.
5 husband   wife
  son   daughter
  uncle   aunt
  grandson   granddaughter
  nephew   niece
  father-in-law mother-in-law

Writing: Joining sentences

2 *Text 1:* I have no brothers or sisters, but I have two cousins. One of them is younger than me and the other one is older. The younger one is 19 and has just started university. The older one is married and lives with her family in Australia.

Text 2: I have two uncles. One is retired and lives in Scotland. The other lives in London and has two children. One is eight and the other is ten.

Unit 3 Talking about places

A Two descriptions

Possible answers:
The bedroom has got a (double) bed, a television and a desk. There's a picture (on the wall above the desk). It's also got a cupboard next to the desk.

In the reception area there's a desk, a low table and there are some chairs. There's a telephone (on the wall). There's a lift.

B Not a good place for a holiday

There's isn't a TV in my room.
My room hasn't got a toilet.
The bathrooms haven't got (any) windows.
There isn't a bar.
There aren't any newspapers or magazines.
There aren't any chairs on the balconies.
The swimming pool hasn't got any water in it!

C Asking questions

1 Has your office got a phone?
2 Have the classrooms got carpets?
3 Has Antarctica got any trees?
4 Is there a university in this town?
5 Are there any mountains in France?
6 Are there any shops in the village?

Listening: Rooms and flats

1 1 A
  2 D
2 *Expected answers:*
  1 This is a small room on the top floor. It's got a bed, a desk, a cupboard and a chair. The bathroom is on the same floor.
  2 This is a large flat on the third floor. It's got a living room, two bedrooms, a kitchen, a bathroom and a small balcony. There isn't a lift. It's by the railway station.

Unit 4 On the move

A Train, bus and plane

I always go by train. It costs £65 return. I usually catch the early morning train. It leaves Kings Cross Station at 6.25 It arrives at Edinburgh at about half past ten. The whole journey takes about four hours.

B Adjectives

1 reliable, uncomfortable
2 crowded, slow
3 cheap, dangerous
4 expensive, comfortable
5 unreliable, empty

C Questions

2 What's the best way to get there?
3 How much does it cost?
4 How long does it take?
5 What time does the train leave?
6 What time does it arrive?
7 How can I get to your house from the station?

Listening: Trip to Stonehenge

Stonehenge is 150 km from London. The best way to go there is by coach. It takes two hours to get there, and costs £32 return.
You can't get there by train because there isn't a station near Stonehenge. You can also rent a car. That costs about £50 a day.

Study pages B

Check your progress

1 *a* by / next to   *d* between
  b above   *e* in front of
  c behind   *f* opposite
2 *a* A (B)   *c* A, B, C
  b D, E   *d* C
3 *a* at six o'clock in the morning
  b on Sunday mornings
  c at midnight on my birthday
4 *a* We haven't got any coffee, but we've got some cakes.
    There isn't any coffee, but there are some cakes.
  b Has this hotel got any single rooms?
    Are there any single rooms in this hotel?

5 I leave home … I catch/take the 6.25 train … arrives in London … I take/catch the underground … I usually get to work … the whole journey takes …

Writing: Punctuation

2 Ernest Hemingway; German; village; today; October; the Alps; summer; London; a language school; Tuesday; the mountains; Can I go now?; the Oxford School of English
3 *a* He speaks German but not Italian.
  b Does this train go to Moscow?
  c The meeting will be on Friday 14th May.
  d Can I get there by bus?
4 My sister has got a new bike and she spends nearly all her time on it. Every afternoon she comes home from school and quickly has something to eat. Then she goes out on her bike and cycles round the streets until it gets dark. I never see her at weekends because she spends all day riding her bike. In the evenings she reads magazines about cycling. It's her birthday next week. Do you know what I'm going to give her? I'm going to give her a mirror for her bike.

Unit 5 Talking about now

A Verb + -ing

Across: 2 going   4 staying
7 making   9 talking   11 getting
14 riding   15 having   16 running
Down: 1 doing   3 lying   5 taking
6 smoking   8 waiting   10 reading
12 washing   13 driving

B There's a woman playing the piano

Possible answers:
3 There are two/some people dancing on a table.
4 There's a man reading a paper.
5 There are some people singing.
6 There's a boy sitting on the floor.
7 There are some people swimming (in the pool).

Listening: We're busy

1 woman and man
2 man
3 woman
4 neither
5 woman
6 woman
7 woman
8 neither

Unit 6 Food and drink

A Ingredients

Other letters: BURGERS AND CHIPS

C A packet of biscuits

1 a packet of tea
2 a jar of coffee
3 a packet/bag of flour
4 a carton of (orange) juice
5 a bottle of wine
7 a can of soup
8 a packet of biscuits
10 a jar of (strawberry) jam

Listening: Polish dishes

1 *Bigos*: tomatoes, cabbage, meat, bacon, spices
  Chlodnik: beetroot, eggs, cream, beetroot leaves
2 chlodnik; chlodnik; bigos; chlodnik

Study pages C

Check your progress

1 *a* He loves (playing) football.
   b He likes (watching) TV.
   c He doesn't mind reading.
   d He doesn't like washing dishes / washing up.
   e He hates washing his hair.
2 usually eat; don't eat; is staying; doesn't eat; eats; aren't eating; are eating.
3 get in/into; get out of
   get on; get off
   get up/get dressed
4 *Possible answers:*
   There's a woman sitting at a table eating spaghetti.
   There's a boy lying on the floor drinking juice.
   There's a girl standing on a chair eating an apple.

Writing: Reference

1 *b* the eggs
   c the man; (in) the house
   d Rome; (to) Rome
2 *a* it; there   *d* them; them; They
   b It; she; it   *e* there; her
   c him; he
3 A new restaurant opened in town last week, so I went there to see what it was like. A waitress came to my table and gave me a menu, but she wasn't very friendly. I ordered chicken and chips. Half an hour later, she brought the food. It wasn't very good. The chicken was tough, and it had a rather strange taste. The chips were cold and greasy. I couldn't eat them at all.
   I called the waitress and asked her to bring me the bill. It came to £25. I asked to see the manager. I told him that I thought £25 was too much for such a bad meal. I gave him £5 and then walked out of the restaurant. I'll never go there again.

Unit 7 The past

A Irregular verbs

Puzzle 1: 1 swam   2 were   3 rode   4 made
Puzzle 2: 1 ▶ was   1 ▼ wrote
2 slept   3 woke   4 left

Puzzle 3: 1 threw   2 had   3 went   4 drank
Puzzle 4: 1 bought   2 sent   3 wore   4 gave   5 taught   6 felt

B Positive and negative

1 Bella had a shower.
2 Dick didn't go to the shops.
3 Bella didn't make a cake.
4 Dick watched television.
5 Bella read the newspaper.
6 Dick lost his umbrella.
7 Bella didn't take the dog for a walk.
8 Bella drove to work.
9 Dick wore a green jumper.

C Asking Wh- questions

2 Where did they go last night?
3 Why did he leave?
4 How much (money) did you spend?
5 What did she say?
6 When did your mother arrive?
7 How did you get in?

Listening: A man and a penguin

1 D B A C
2 *a* outside his front door
   b the police station
   c take the penguin to the zoo
   d the man and the penguin at a bus stop
   e take that penguin to the zoo
   f to the zoo
   g we're going to the cinema

Unit 8 A place to live

A Phrases

2 a view of the sea
3 faces north
4 a main road
5 looks out on a park
6 block of flats
7 the ninth floor

B What are they like?

2 noisy   6 dark
3 sunny/light 7 quiet
4 untidy   8 spacious
5 convenient   9 dirty

C Things in rooms

A bedroom   B kitchen
C bathroom   D living room

2 There's a poster
3 in the corner
4 There's a cooker
5 on the shelf (above the fridge)
6 There's a fridge
7 next to the toilet
8 There's a rug
9 on the wall (above the washbasin)
10 There are some/three cushions
11 behind the sofa
12 There's a vase

Listening: Favourite rooms

1 It's a large room. It has an old sofa. The shelf is full of CDs and cassettes. The speakers are very large. I listen to loud music.
2 It's very small. It's bright and sunny. It has a wooden bed. The shelf has toys on it. The chair is by the window.

Study pages D

Check your progress

1 *a* Both (of them) are wearing glasses.
   b Neither (of them) has long hair.
   c One (of them) is wearing a hat and the other isn't wearing a hat.
2 *b* last Saturday / last weekend / six days ago
   c this morning / earlier today / a few hours ago
   d in March / six months ago
   e the day before yesterday / two days ago
3 A I went to London
   B Did you have a good time?
   A it was very interesting
   B Where did you stay?
   A I stayed in a friend's flat
   B And what did you do?
   A Well, my friend took me … we didn't see the Queen
4 *a* block; floor; looks
   b main; noisy; convenient
   c faces; sunny/light; view

Writing: Joining ideas

2 *a* but   *c* but   *e* and
   b so   *d* so
3 A
4 *Possible answer:*
   I've got a new flat. It has a living room, a bedroom and a small kitchen. It's near the town centre,

but it's a long way from the main road, so it's not too noisy. It's also near the beach, and it has a beautiful view of the sea.

Unit 9 I've done it!

A What's the rule?

1 opened		8	bought
2 washed		9	written
3 sold		10	cut
4 got		11	arrived
5 put		12	spoken
6 had		13	left
7 broken		14	gone

Rule: have or has + *past participle*

B I'm ready!

1 They've put on some music.
  They've cooked a meal.
2 She's bought her ticket.
  She's packed her case.
  She's found her passport.
3 They've cleaned their teeth.
  They've got into bed.
  They've said 'Goodnight'.

C Positive and negative

2 She's painted a picture.
  She hasn't taken a photo.
3 They've got married.
  They haven't got divorced.
4 He's drunk his lemonade.
  He hasn't eaten his sandwich.
5 They've won the game.
  They haven't lost the game.

Listening: What has happened?

1D, 2A, 3C, 4B
1 *a* He's lost his glasses.
  b They're on the table.
2 *a* She's got engaged.
  b They were on holiday in Spain.
3 *a* She's sold her car.
  b She goes everywhere by bike.
4 *a* She's broken her arm.
  b She fell off her bike.

Unit 10 Clothes

A What are they wearing?

1 She's wearing a blouse, earrings, a skirt and (high-heeled) shoes.
2 He's wearing a uniform, black boots and glasses.

3 She's wearing a jumper, jeans and sandals.
4 He's wearing a T-shirt, shorts, trainers and sunglasses.
5 She's wearing a hat, a coat, a scarf, boots and gloves.
6 He's wearing a shirt, a tie, a jacket, trousers and shoes.

B Buying clothes

2 Can I try it on?
3 Here you are.
4 How does it look?
5 It looks very good.
6 It really suits you.
7 Does it feel OK?
8 It fits very well.
9 How much is it?
10 That's not too expensive.

Listening: Working clothes

1 1B: jeans, T-shirt, jumper, jacket
  2C: skirt, blouse, dress, trousers
  3A: suit, shirt, tie, black shoes, socks
2 Speaker 1 works at home, sometimes goes to meetings.
  Speaker 2 sells computer equipment, visits customers.
  Speaker 3 works in a bank.

Study pages E

Check your progress

1 *a* Mine; Alan's
  b theirs; Ours
2 *a* I've written; I wrote
  b Did you go
  c Has he woken up; He woke up
  d She hasn't come
3 *a* has
  b possessive
  c is
4 I've packed my case
  I've found our passports
  Have you packed your case?
  I haven't washed my hair
  Has she phoned?
  She's bought the tickets
  she hasn't collected them yet
5 *Possible answers:*
  a shorts, trainers, T-shirt
  b hat, gloves, boots
  c necklace, earrings, ring

Writing: Sequence (1)

1 *a* then; after that; first
  b and then; and
2 *Possible answer:*
  First I collect the children from school. Then I take them to the park, and then we come home and we have supper together. After that I play with them for an hour, and then they have a bath and get ready for bed. Then I read them a story. After that I can sit down and relax.

Unit 11 Quantity

A A, some and any

1 some		5 any		9	an
2 some		6 a		10	some
3 any		7 a		11	some
4 a		8 a		12	any

B Quantity expressions

Possible answers:
2 There are very few people in Antarctica.
3 There are lots of cars in Los Angeles.
4 Nurses don't earn much money.
5 There's hardly any rain in the Sahara Desert.
6 A lot of people speak Spanish.
7 Bill Gates has got plenty of money.
8 There aren't any colour photos in this book.

C Too and enough

Possible answers:
1 They give me too much work.
2 There isn't enough time.
3 We don't get enough holidays.
4 They don't pay me enough money.
5 There aren't enough young people.
6 There are too many old people.
7 There aren't enough things to do.

Listening: A healthy diet

1 *Possible scores:*

	Speaker 1	Speaker 2
sweet things	2	4
fat	3	5
vegetables	4	2
fruit	5	3
meat	1	5
fish	3	0

2 Speaker 1

Unit 12 How do you feel?

A Where does it hurt?

1	head	6	feet
2	wrist	7	back
3	arm	8	stomach
4	chest	9	tooth
5	knee	10	shoulder

In the bottle: Paracetamol

C The right medicine

1 pain/ache
2 aspirins/paracetamols/pills
3 felt
4 appointment
5 examined
6 prescription
7 chemist/chemist's
8 prescription
9 trousers/jeans

Listening: Ouch!

1 A1 Her neck aches/hurts.
  B3 She's got a headache.
  C2 Her knee hurts.

2 *a* 3	*d* 2	*g* 2
b 2	*e* 3	*h* 3
c 1	*f* 1	*i* 1

Study pages F

Check your progress

1 *a* Ed has lived in London since 1980.
  b He has worked for Barclays Bank since 1982.
  c Ed and Laura have been married since 1990.
  d They've had a house for five years.
  e They've had a computer for six months.
2 *a* some; any
  b There are; too many; there's; too much
  c very few; very little
3 I've got a pain in my arm.
  My shoulder hurts/aches.
  I've got an ache in my leg.
  I've got a headache.

Writing: Lists

2 *a* I really enjoyed the party. The food was delicious, there was lots of good music and I met some very interesting people.

b I don't like my flat-mate much. She never cleans the flat and she plays loud music all the time. Also, she has some very strange friends.
3 *Possible answers*:
  a The streets are full of traffic and there's nowhere to park. Also, the shops are very crowded.
  b It's just the right length, it's a very unusual colour and it goes with your eyes.
  c Her legs ached, her feet hurt and she felt tired and hungry.
  d It's very clean and the food's always freshly cooked. Also, it's not too expensive.

Unit 13 What will happen?

A Will and won't

1 He won't remember his sister's birthday.
2 She'll fail her exams.
  She won't pass her exams.
3 He'll miss the bus.
  He won't catch the bus.
4 He'll lose the match.
  He won't win the match.
5 She won't go to the concert.
  She'll stay at home.

B Questions with 'will'

3 What time / When will the train arrive?
4 Will it be windy tomorrow?
5 Will there be food at the party?
6 Where will you be tomorrow afternoon?
7 When will I see you again?
8 Will she pass her exam?
9 How much will the tickets cost?

Listening: Giving blood

1 Nothing. Just lie down and relax.
2 About half a litre.
3 No – maybe a bit when the needle goes in.
4 About half an hour altogether.
5 A bit weak at first, then normal.

Unit 14 About town

A Places to go (1)

1 café, restaurant, bar
2 church, mosque, cathedral
3 disco, nightclub
4 art gallery, museum
5 zoo
6 theatre, cinema, concert hall
7 castle
8 sports centre, stadium, park, swimming pool

C Giving directions

Possible answers:
1 Go under the bridge, and then go straight on across the river, past the park, and turn left at the end of the road. The university is on the left.
2 Yes. Go straight on down this road, and turn right at the church. You'll see the swimming pool on the left.

Listening: Living in London

1 *a* W	*c* W	*e* M
b M	*d* M	

2 *Possible answers*:
  b He can walk to the theatre in 15 minutes.
  c There are trains and planes, so it's very noisy.
  d He meets his friends in cafés.
  e It feels like a big city.

Study pages G

Check your progress

1 *a* I'll phone (you) when I get to the airport.
  b When I get to the hotel I'll send (you) a postcard.

c I'll phone (you) if anything happens.

d If you don't phone, I'll phone the hotel.

2 *a* Yes, she does. No, she doesn't.

b Yes, they have. No, they haven't.

c Yes, it will. No, it won't.

3 *b* I'll probably …

c There might be …

d The world probably won't …

e We won't …

4 *Possible answer*:

You go along this road, past the school, and turn right. Then you go over the bridge and turn left at the cinema. You'll see the museum on your left.

Writing: Reason and contrast

2 *a* Although   *c* but; so

b As/Because   *d* so; but

3 *Possible answers*:

a It's a small town, so it's easy to get to know people, and everyone is very friendly.

b Because the town has five factories, the air is very polluted, so it's a very unhealthy place to live.

c Although it's a large industrial town and it's quite ugly, I like living there because it has a very friendly atmosphere.

d It's only a small town, but there's lots to do in the evenings, and as it's by the sea it's very popular with tourists.

Unit 15 Comparing things

A Yes, but …

3 (Thailand)'s hotter.

4 (Chinese) is more difficult.

5 (Barcelona) is better.

6 (*Bright Eyes*) is more beautiful.

7 (frogs) are uglier.

8 there are more people in (India).

B Opposites

1 Silver is *cheaper* than gold.

2 University students are *older* than schoolchildren.

3 Plastic is *lighter* than metal.

4 Arizona is *drier* than California.

5 Reading is *easier* than listening.

6 Europe is *richer* than Africa.

7 Mars is *colder* than Venus.

C World records

2 China has got the largest population in the world.

3 Russia is the largest country …

4 The whale is the largest animal …

5 The cheetah is the fastest animal …

6 The Nile is the longest river …

7 Everest is the highest mountain …

Listening: The most and the fewest

1 *a* B   *b* A   *c* A   *d* B

2 *a* A

b A (and possibly C)

c C

3 *a* B (Spanish)

b B and C

c none of them

Unit 16 Free time

A Things people do

Possible answers:

Carol: She collects coins and shells, (and she also collects stamps.)

Jane: She likes jazz, she plays the violin (and she also sings in a band.)

Jim: He enjoys reading science fiction and poetry, (and he reads three newspapers every day.)

Leo: He plays chess and cards, (and he plays lots of computer games.)

Flo: She does a lot of knitting and painting, (and she loves cooking.)

Bill: He often goes climbing and cycling, (and he enjoys walking.)

B Sports

1 race	9 ▶ game
2 track	9 ▼ goal
3 ride	10 hole
4 ▶ players	11 kick
4 ▼ points	12 throw
5 basket	13 rackets
6 club	14 hit
7 ball	15 net
8 drive	

Listening: Rock climbing

1 a, d, e

2 Picture B.

Expected answers:

'I'm going to hurt myself.'

'The rope's going to break.'

Check your progress

1 *a* He's very good at playing the guitar.

b I'm quite good at cooking.

c She's not very good at (speaking) French.

d They're no good at remembering other people's names.

2 *a* Flies have fewer legs than spiders.

b Motorbikes use less petrol than cars.

3 *a* went for

b go; go for; play

c goes; goes

d playing

4 *a* the most popular

b friendlier

c more difficult

d the highest

Writing: Sequence (2)

2 *a* I first met him at a party in London. About a year later I met him again.

b She put the phone down. After a few seconds, she picked it up again and dialled a number.

3 *Possible answers*:

a and; A few minutes later; and

b and; After half an hour

c First; Then; and; About an hour later

4 Monica knew exactly what to do. She wrote a letter and put it on the table. The letter said 'Goodbye, Edward. I've had enough.' Then she packed a small suitcase and called a taxi. After about ten minutes the taxi arrived. Monica closed the door and posted her keys through the letter box. Two hours later Edward arrived home.

Unit 17 Rules and advice

A Children's questions

Possible answers:

1 Can we watch (the) cartoons?

2 Can we have burger and chips?
Do we have to have Irish stew?

3 Do they have to go home?
Can they stay?

4 Can we finish our game?
Do we have to go to bed?

5 Can I do my homework later?
  Do I have to do it now?
6 Do I have to go to school?
  Can I stay at home?

B Must and have to

Theatre: You have to (must) pay to go in. You don't have to wear very smart clothes.
Train: You have to (must) have a ticket with you. You don't have to stay in your seat. You mustn't put your feet on the seats. You mustn't throw things out of the window.
Beach: You don't have to pay to go into the water. You have to (must) put your rubbish in the bin. You don't have to sit in the sun. You mustn't park on the beach.

C Giving advice

2 you should visit the dentist regularly, you shouldn't eat too many sweets, (and you should clean your teeth twice a day.)
3 you should wear a seat belt, you shouldn't use a mobile phone, (and you shouldn't go too fast.)
4 you should dress smartly, you shouldn't arrive late, (and you should be polite.)
5 you should do lots of exercise, you shouldn't eat fatty food, (and you should eat plenty of fruit.)

Listening: Radio phone-in

1 Susan has a job, and she has a problem with her husband, who has just got a new job. In the evening he wants to stay at home and watch TV (and sleep). She wants to go out. But he won't go out with her.
2 *a* 1   *d* 1   *f* 2
  b –   *e* –   *g* –
  c 2

Unit 18 A day's work

A Jobs

2 He's a lorry driver. He delivers heavy goods.
3 She's a dentist. She looks after people's teeth.
4 He's a hairdresser. He cuts people's hair.
5 She's an accountant. She manages people's money.

6 He's a mechanic. He repairs cars.
7 She's a housewife. She looks after her family.
8 He's a receptionist. He deals with enquiries.
9 She's a journalist. She writes news stories.
10 He's a disc jockey. He plays dance music.

C One job after another

2 he studied economics at university
3 he got a job in a department store
4 they promoted him to advertising manager
5 he left his job
6 he taught English in a language school
7 he got the sack
8 he applied for a lot of jobs
9 he saw an advertisement for a job
10 he went for an interview
11 he got the job
12 Joe became a lorry driver

Listening: A security guard

1 Security guards work for companies.
  Their job is to guard buildings. They stop people breaking into the building.
2 *a* No   *d* No   *f* No
  b Yes *e* Yes *g* No
  c No

Study pages I

Check your progress

1 *a* somewhere
  b anywhere; anyone
  c something
  d someone
2 *a* looks after *d* applied for
  b deals with   *e* pay for
  c work for
3 *a* You have to/must …
     You mustn't/can't …
  b You can …
     You don't have to …
  c You mustn't/can't …
     You have to/must …
4 *a* hours; salary; meet; travel
  b sack; promote

Writing: Letter writing

2 *a* Elizabeth Burke
  b Don

c Douglas Trafford
d Miranda

Unit 19 Telling stories

A What were they doing?

Possible answers:
2 We were in a restaurant. We were having dinner.
3 I was running in the park.
4 I was in the car. I was driving home from work.
5 We were at a nightclub. We were dancing.
6 I was in the kitchen. I was cooking dinner.
7 We were in a bar. We were having a drink.

B What happened next?

Possible answers:
2 While Peter was cleaning his teeth in the bathroom, the lights went out. (He waited a few minutes and they came on again.)
3 Sam was opening his front door when the key broke. (So he climbed in through the window.)
4 While Tony and Linda were walking by the river, they saw a man's coat in the water. (Then they saw a body in the water.)

C Can you remember?

Possible answers:
Lake: He was in a boat fishing, wearing a green jacket and a hat.
Pool: He was lying on a towel, holding a drink and talking to a woman.
Theatre: He was waiting to buy tickets, carrying a bunch of flowers.
Station: He was getting on to the train carrying a suitcase and wearing a coat.

Listening: The wedding video

1 About 100.
2 He was a photographer.
3 He walked around the hotel, made a video.
4 Coats. Some people left money.
5 The money was missing.
6 One of his wife's cousins.
7 He was on the video.
8 They showed him the video.

Unit 20 People

A Who's who?

1	D	6	C	11	C
2	B	7	C	12	B
3	A	8	D	13	D
4	C	9	A	14	A
5	D	10	B		

B People on a train

Possible answers:
Woman: She was in her 20s. She was quite tall and she had short fair hair. She was wearing a green dress and sunglasses.
Man: He was a bald man in his 70s, with a short grey beard and blue eyes. He had a walking stick.

C Character adjectives

2	mean	7	easy-going
3	bad-tempered	8	lazy
4	shy	9	generous
5	hard-working	10	forgetful
6	honest	11	selfish

Listening: Family picture

1 Uncle: C   Cousin: A
  Aunt: D   Aunt Sophie: F
  Grandfather: I
2 *a* His uncle is a dentist / is rich.
  b His aunt is a dentist.
  c His grandfather is 88 / lives a few streets away.
  d His cousin is a musician / is in Japan / is learning to play Japanese music.
  e His aunt Sophie is his father's sister / lives in Miami / is the manager of a hotel.

Study pages J

Check your progress

1 *a* Mexican   *d* Brazilian
  b Greek   *e* Polish
  c Japanese
2 *Possible answers*:
  a during lunch
     while we were having lunch
  b during the night
     while I was asleep/sleeping
3 *Possible answer*:
  Last night, Sam was watching TV in his bedroom when he heard a noise in the garden. He went to the window and looked outside. He saw two men climbing over the garden wall. One of them was holding a gun.
4 *Possible answers*:
  a … a woman in her 20s with long wavy dark hair, wearing a big hat and earrings.
  b … a bald man in his 70s with a long nose and a grey beard.

Writing: Relative clauses (1)

2 *a* I live in Stenton, which is a small village near Cambridge.
  b I've got three sisters, who are all older than me.
  c Pandas, which only eat bamboo, are becoming very rare.
3 *a* which was built in the 70s
  b who are also staying in Paris
  c which is a kind of sausage
  d which is about 200 km south of here
  e who's studying art here
  f which still isn't very good

Unit 21 Future plans

A New Year resolutions

Possible answers:
I'm going to smile.
I'm going to take my family out.
I'm going to visit my friends.
I'm not going to spend all my money on myself.
I'm going to buy presents for my children.
I'm not going to drink too much alcohol.
I'm not going to watch too much TV.
I'm not going to use my mobile phone in restaurants.
I'm going to have a shower every day.

B The ghost comes back

Possible answers:
This evening, the Browns are coming for dinner.
Tomorrow morning he's going to the hairdresser's.
Tomorrow evening he's attending a school concert.
The day after tomorrow he's having lunch with his parents-in-law.
On Friday, he's giving a birthday party for his daughter.
Next week, his brother and family are coming to stay.
In two months, he's taking the family for a holiday at the seaside.

Listening: Plans for the evening

1 A 3, 4   C 1, (3, 4)
  B 1   D 2, 5
2 a 4, b 5, c 1, d 2

Unit 22 Around the world

A Where are they?

Possible answers:
2 Finland is a country in northern Europe, which has a border with Russia.
3 Chile is a long narrow country on the west coast of South America.
4 Panama is a very small country in Central America, which has an Atlantic and a Pacific coast.
5 Egypt is a country in North Africa, on the Mediterranean Sea.

B On the map

1	ocean	6	mountain
2	border	7	lake
3	island	8	volcano
4	coast	9	forest
5	river	10	desert

Missing word: continents

Listening: Living in a hot climate

1 Yes
2 July and August
3 – (doesn't say)
4 No
5 – (doesn't say)
6 Yes
7 No (they're air-conditioned)
8 Yes (in air-conditioned buildings)
9 No (not in summer)

Study pages K

Check your progress

1 *a* There was no one …
  b They didn't eat anything …
  c You're not going anywhere.
  d I've got (I have) no money.
2 *a* 3   *b* 1   *c* 2   *d* 2   *e* 3
3 *a* They aren't going to get up early (… going to go to work).
  b Jill isn't going to type letters.
  c Tim isn't going to wear a suit.
  d They're going to lie in the sun.
  e Tim's going to read magazines.
  f Jill's going to swim.
4 *a* Europe; Asia; South America; Africa
  b Ocean; Sea
  c population

Writing: Relative clauses (2)

1 *a* Jakarta, which is the capital of Indonesia, has …
  b The Cape Verde Islands, which were once a Portuguese colony, have been …
  c … of Charles I, who was King of England from 1625 to 1649.
2 *Possible answer*:
  If you have time, you should visit the Parrot Café, which is in a small side street behind the harbour. It's the oldest café in the town and it's very popular with fishermen, who sit there all day playing cards. The owner, who is in his 80s, is a retired sea captain. Next to the Parrot Café there's a small museum, where you can see treasure from an old sailing ship, which sank near the town in the 17th century.

Unit 23 Past and present

A Everything has changed

1 *c* She's started wearing glasses.
  d She's bought a new computer.
2 *a* They've got married.
  b They've moved to London.
  c They've had children / a child.
  d Julia's stopped working.
3 *a* He's come out of prison.
  b He's grown a moustache.
  c He's shaved off his beard.
  d He's finished his book.

B The answer's 'No'

2 Has she gone yet?
3 Have they got up yet?
4 Have you found your (key) yet?
5 Has he come home/in yet?
6 Have you finished your book yet?
7 Has the bus come yet?
8 Has he got married yet?
9 Have they moved yet?

Listening: Have you ever …?

1 Have you ever ridden a motorbike?
  Have you ever been sailing?
  Have you ever eaten ostrich?
  Have you ever seen a play by Shakespeare?
2 1 *a* 15
    b He started the engine. He didn't tell her how to stop.
    c Very frightened.
  2 *a* 10
    b His uncle and aunt.
    c Sunny, not too much wind.

3 *a* Ostrich burgers.
  b Very good – between chicken and beef.
  c About once a week.
4 *a* *Hamlet*.
  b Last weekend.
  c It was good. She enjoyed it.

Unit 24 Arts and entertainment

A Who, what and where?

2 band
3 soap
4 orchestra
5 play
6 news
7 channels
8 director
9 museum
10 exhibition
11 comedy
12 musician
13 actress
14 concert
15 song
16 composer
17 film
18 writer
19 documentary
20 gallery
21 stars
22 actor
23 sport
24 quiz
25 opera
26 poet
27 singer

Listening: TV survey

1 *a* 2   *c* 1   *e* –
  b 4   *d* –   *f* 5
2 *a* 5. If there's a war in Africa it often isn't on the news.
  b 1. There's plenty of ordinary pop music on TV.
  c 3. On Saturday afternoon all you can watch is sport.
  d 4. Foreign films are usually on late at night.
  e 2. The news programmes on TV aren't very interesting for teenagers.

Final review

Sentences

1 Has this hotel got a restaurant?
2 I bought/got this car ten years ago.
3 They've lived/been in London since 1990.
4 Our TV was more expensive than theirs.
5 We didn't go anywhere.
6 You don't have to get up.

Lists

1 uncle; niece
2 lamb, pork
3 *Four of:* tomato, onion, carrot, mushroom, garlic, pepper

4 shirt, shorts, boots, sunglasses
5 skirt, gloves, shoes, necklace
6 *Four of:* generous, selfish, mean, friendly, easy-going, lazy, honest

Verbs

1 enjoys; doesn't play; love; don't like
2 writes; is writing
3 see; 'll invite
4 's had; 's got; hasn't drunk
5 was driving; ran; didn't hit
6 've never eaten; 've eaten; had
7 'm going ('m going to go)

Words in context

1 meet; fall; get
2 leaves; arrives; journey/trip
3 block; faces; view
4 size; try; suits
5 kick; throw; hit
6 sack; promote
7 Europe; border; Ocean

Questions

1 How many televisions have you got?
2 How long does it take?
3 When did she leave?
4 Has he finished work yet?
5 How will they get to the station?
6 Will there be a test on Friday?
7 Do we have to pay to go in?
8 Where are they going to stay?
9 What are you having for lunch?
10 Have you ever been to Toronto?

Prepositions

1 by
2 on; at; in
3 by
4 on; past; on
5 along/up/down; in; with
6 of; for
7 for (in); with; after
8 in; on
9 at
10 during/in

Tables

1 noisy/loud; untidy
  dirty; light (sunny)
2 Italian; German
  Chinese; Spanish
3 left; left
  took; taken
  came; come
4 friendlier; friendliest
  more popular; most popular
  better; best

Irregular verbs

Infinitive	Simple past	Past participle
be	was/were	been
become	became	become
bite	bit	bitten
blow	blew	blown
break	broke	broken
bring	brought	brought
build	built	built
buy	bought	bought
can	could	(been able)
catch	caught	caught
choose	chose	chosen
come	came	come
cost	cost	cost
cut	cut	cut
do	did	done
draw	drew	drawn
dream	dreamt	dreamt
drink	drank	drunk
drive	drove	driven
eat	ate	eaten
fall	fell	fallen
feed	fed	fed
feel	felt	felt
find	found	found
fly	flew	flown
forget	forgot	forgotten
get	got	got
give	gave	given
go	went	gone (been)
have	had	had
hear	heard	heard
hide	hid	hidden
hit	hit	hit
hold	held	held
hurt	hurt	hurt
keep	kept	kept
know	knew	known
lay	laid	laid
learn	learnt	learnt
leave	left	left
lend	lent	lent
let	let	let
lie	lay	lain
lose	lost	lost
make	made	made
mean	meant	meant
meet	met	met
pay	paid	paid
put	put	put
read /riːd/	read /red/	read /red/
ride	rode	ridden
ring	rang	rung
rise	rose	risen
run	ran	run
say	said	said
see	saw	seen
sell	sold	sold
send	sent	sent
set	set	set
shake	shook	shaken
shine	shone	shone
shoot	shot	shot
show	showed	shown
shut	shut	shut
sing	sang	sung
sit	sat	sat
sleep	slept	slept
speak	spoke	spoken
spell	spelt	spelt
spend	spent	spent
stand	stood	stood
steal	stole	stolen
swim	swam	swum
take	took	taken
teach	taught	taught
tear	torn	torn
think	thought	thought
throw	threw	thrown
understand	understood	understood
wake	woke	woken
wear	wore	worn
win	won	won
write	wrote	written

Phonetic symbols

Vowels

Symbol	Example
/iː/	tree /triː/
/i/	many /ˈmeni/
/ɪ/	sit /sɪt/
/e/	bed /bed/
/æ/	back /bæk/
/ʌ/	sun /sʌn/
/ɑː/	car /kɑː/
/ɒ/	hot /hɒt/
/ɔː/	horse /hɔːs/
/ʊ/	full /fʊl/
/uː/	moon /muːn/
/ɜː/	girl /gɜːl/
/ə/	arrive /əˈraɪv/
	water /ˈwɔːtə/
/eɪ/	late /leɪt/
/aɪ/	time /taɪm/
/ɔɪ/	boy /bɔɪ/
/əʊ/	home /həʊm/
/aʊ/	out /aʊt/
/ɪə/	here /hɪə/
/eə/	there /ðeə/
/ʊə/	pure /pjʊə/

Consonants

Symbol	Example
/p/	pull /pʊl/
/b/	bad /bæd/
/t/	take /teɪk/
/d/	dog /dɒg/
/k/	cat /kæt/
/g/	go /gəʊ/
/tʃ/	church /tʃɜːtʃ/
/dʒ/	age /eɪdʒ/
/f/	for /fɔː/
/v/	love /lʌv/
/θ/	thick /θɪk/
/ð/	this /ðɪs/
/s/	sit /sɪt/
/z/	zoo /zuː/
/ʃ/	shop /ʃɒp/
/ʒ/	leisure /ˈleʒə/
/h/	house /haʊs/
/m/	make /meɪk/
/n/	name /neɪm/
/ŋ/	bring /brɪŋ/
/l/	look /lʊk/
/r/	road /rəʊd/
/j/	young /jʌŋ/
/w/	wear /weə/

Stress

We show stress by a mark (/ˈ/) before the stressed syllable:
later /ˈleɪtə/; arrive /əˈraɪv/; information /ɪnfəˈmeɪʃn/.

Acknowledgements

The authors and publishers are grateful to the following illustrators and photographers:

Illustrators: Kathy Baxendale: pp. 16 *t*, 30 *br*, 31; Linda Combi: p. 39; Rachel Deacon: pp. 15, 16 *b*, 19, 22, 28, 34, 44 *bl*, 61, 67 *bl*, 76 *br*; Nick Duffy: pp. 35 *bl*, 41 *bl*, 42, 43 *m*, 64, 68 *ml*, *bl*, 80 *br*, 81 *tr*; Belinda Evans: pp. 17, 26 *tl*, 32 *tl*, 36, 37, 54, 60, 66 *tr*, 76 *l*, 77; Gecko DTP: pp. 12, 21, 42 *tr*, 50 *bl*, 62 *l*, 72 *l*, 81 *ml*; Jo Goodberry: pp. 18, 49; Jackie Harland: pp. 24, 25, 53; Phil Healey: pp. 10, 23 *bl*, 26 *bl*, 29, 35 *t*, 38 *bl*, 40 *mbr*, 43 *tr*, 52, 58, 67 *tr*; Rosalind Hudson: pp. 12 *border*, 23 *tl*, 57 *mr*, 80 *bl*; Paul McCaffrey: p. 66 *m*; Louise Morgan: pp. 33, 48, 51, 57 *b*; Pantelis Palios: pp. 11, 30 *mr*, 40 *mtr*, 41 *t*, 45, 65 *bl*, 70; Sam Thompson: p. 55; Kath Walker: pp. 14, 20 *r*, 26 *r*, 32 *r*, 38 *r*, 44 *r*, 50 *r*, 56, 62 *r*, 68 *r*, 74.

Photographers: Eye Ubiquitous/G. Daniels: p. 47; The Photographers Library: pp. 19 & 37; Popperfoto: p. 56; Jules Selmes: pp. 25, 36.

t = top   *m* = middle   *b* = bottom   *r* = right   *l* = left

Cover design by Dunne & Scully.

Design, production and repro handled by Gecko Limited, Bicester, Oxon.

Sound recordings by Martin Williamson, Prolingua Productions at Studio AVP.

Freelance editorial work by Meredith Levy.